That is the author candidly admits that this self-help book is directly influenced plus inspired by the Books of Amos, Daniel, and Proverbs--scribed by Solomon, monarch son and heir of David, the "giant slayer".

Although each character is undeniably a biblical-theological figure, they were most effective and impacted their encompassing secular world, one singular sphere at-a-time. In brief, this text is fresh perspective on a biblical narrative; however, from a 21st Century academic context.

Professor Bonet is a Decorated Persian Gulf War Veteran. He has served in both Operation Desert Shield and Desert Storm.

Also, the author is a member and supporter of Disabled American Veterans, American Legion of Veterans, and Veterans of Foreign Wars.

QUANTUM

Acad(ynaE3)mics^SM:

Unveiling the Dynamic Force of the Predictive Mind

An intermediate-level
self-help book concerning
the limitless power of a
meta-cognitive mind

—1st Edition—

Prof Claude E. Bonet

Order this book online at www.trafford.com
or email orders@trafford.com

Most Trafford titles are also available at major online book retailers.

Printed in the United States of America.

ISBN: 978-1-4669-9710-3 (sc)
ISBN: 978-1-4669-9709-7 (e)

Trafford rev. 08/09/2013

www.trafford.com

North America & international
toll-free: 1 888 232 4444 (USA & Canada)
fax: 812 355 4082

I dedicate this comprehensive strategic system guide-blueprint to my wife "Cedrina Patrice K". For your endless years of devotion plus untiring self-sacrifice. I could not have completed this 12 year journey without your being at my side and having my back. I appreciate you And are forever grateful. You are priceless! My friend and soulmate.

"Ille Ingenuae Praedictum"

CONTENTS

You may contact the author for speaking engagements at the following avenues:

1) LiveJournal: https://livejournal.com/profcebonet2020;
2) Email: HYPERLINK "mailto:claude.e.bonet2020@gmail.com" \t "_blank" claude.e.bonet2020@gmail.com;
3) Twitter: Search for 'Prof Claude Bonet';
4) MySpace: https://new.myspace.com/profclaudeebonet.

QUADRANT I

Fundamental Field of the Invention:

The present invention relates generally to a method, apparatus and system. More specifically, the present invention is a new method and system for higher education.

Background of the Invention:

This mixed methods study is comprised of five core quadrants, with quadrant four however being the main body. It is sub-divided into eight aspects. There are a total of four research questions. The overarching framework involves the limitless dividends of intuition and perception, and the benefit plus value of pain and suffering. The primary hypothesis is that the skillful integration of the Quantum Acad(yna^{E3})mics$^{SM®}$ Strategic System into conventional solution plans; it will result in increased overall efficacy. It will serve as a reliable plan that thoroughly responds to diverse crises confronting society at-large. The secondary hypothesis will irrefutably confirm and reinforce the necessity for integrating intuitive abilities and practices into already implemented critical thinking solution plans. The null hypothesis, conversely, nullifies and refutes the notion that there is a negative correlation between the presence of intuition within already implemented solution plans, and its lack of affecting the results one way or the other. The design and methodology endeavors, firstly—qualitative study—to explore and understand the meaning individuals or groups ascribe to a social or human problem (Creswell, 2009, p. 4). Secondly, it assesses—quantitative study—measures, and tests—objective theories by examining the relationships among variables (Creswell, 2009, p. 4). The main strategy of inquiry which will be utilized is the Concurrent Transformative Strategy. It is a combination of the

Concurrent Triangulation Strategy, as well as the Concurrent Embedded Strategy. These strategies will be discussed later, in greater detail. In brief, the mixed methods strategy is an integration of the qualitative and quantitative research methods.

The sources and data collection includes, firstly, the sample audience—adult-level students plus educational administration and faculty. It includes professionals from the disciplines of counseling-psychology, social sciences, and military, as well as science plus technology agencies-organizations. In brief, surveys and questionnaires will be forwarded to hand-selected individuals at places of employment; it will also include various conferences, lectures, and symposiums. The potential-anticipated result(s) section asserts that substantive information will be gathered. Information that will confirm, validate, and verify that if the proposed system is skillfully integrated and reinforced within conventional solution plans, a majority of impending crises will be reversed, or perhaps even wholly averted.

Brief Description of the Drawings:

FIG. 1 is a flowchart of Charbonnet's rudimentary Layout of the "Quantum Acad(yna^{E3}) mics$^{SM®}$ Blueprint Schematics Plan", the Main Pillars

FIG. 2 is a flowchart of the "Trinity of manKind" in the present invention.

FIG. 3 is a flowchart of Charbonnet's "Action-Consequence" Logical Expression in the present invention.

FIG. 4 is a diagram of a Model of Transformational Leadership in the present invention.

FIG. 5 is a table predicting the correlation between Leader LPC Scores and Group Effectiveness according to Fielder's Contingency Model in the present invention.

FIG. 6 is a flowchart of Applicable Virtues from Patterson's Model in the present invention.

Detail of the Novel Learning Concept:

All illustrations of the drawings are for the purpose of describing selected versions of the present invention and are not intended to limit the scope of the present invention. Higher education (herein referenced as HE) intends to revolutionize the hearts and minds of its target—administrative, faculty, and student—population. HE intends to provoke transformation, via the facilitation and utilization (herein referenced as FNU) of diverse instruments-tools—assessments, courseroom curricula, instructional guides plus manuals, surveys, and questionnaires; this also includes the internet and social media forums, for example. The core objective is the manifestation of lasting comprehensive maturation—change, development, and growth (herein referenced as CDNG). If facilitated effectively, the end result is the manifestation of five core tenets or disciplines of the typical leadership agency: 1. Systems thinking; 2. Personal mastery; 3. Mental models; 4. Building shared vision; 5. Team learning ("The Jossey-Bass Reader", 2007, pp. 6-9). In brief, higher education endeavors to aid the appropriate citizens thereof in abolishing and destroying the illusion that the world at-large is created of separate, 5 unrelated forces ("The Jossey-Bass Reader", 2007, p. 1). Adult-level academics ought to be established upon a chief cornerstone, referred simply as "enhancing adult motivation to learn" (Wlodkowski, 2008, p. 4). Wlodkowski citing Paley (2008) asserts that "None of us are to be found in sets of tasks or lists of attributes; we can be known only in the unfolding of our unique stories within the context of everyday events" (p. 1).

In other words, adult education's core mission (herein referenced as CM) is helping students—individually and collectively—achieve their goals and aspirations (Merriam et al. citing McClure, 2006, p. xi). The encompassing purpose (herein referenced as EP) thereof involves aiding, assisting, and equipping of responsible citizens foster development and greatly enhancing the quality of living within their communities (Merriam et al. citing McClure, 2006, p. xi). These individuals understand that they possess a distinct role within the agency of the collective individual (herein referenced as ACI). This role comprises him-herself, as a member of the public and as a participant in economic, social, and political activities that extend from participation in the market to direct or indirect intervention in individual or joint activities in political and other types of terrain (Merriam et al., 2006, p. 25). In brief, the overarching purpose is the raising up of a next-generation of competent, effective and highly skilled critical thinkers (herein referenced as CT) plus solution originators (herein referenced as SO), all prepared in serving as agents of socio-cultural, economic, and philosophic reformation and transformation.

Brookfield (1987) reinforces the preceding; hence professing that "Learning to think critically is one of the most significant activities of adult life" (p. ix). When adults engage therein the quest for advanced-level critical thinking, they develop an awareness of the assumptions under which individuals act, function, and think (Brookfield, 1987, p. ix). Nonetheless, the chief advantage of embracing and enhancing critical analytics (herein referenced as CA)—pertinent to assumptions of self-actions and others, is organizationally and culturally beneficial, as well as personally liberating (Brookfield, 1987, p. 43). Brookfield citing Fromm (1987) remarks "the prospect of freedom without reason is enough to drive us into psychical, physical, and political enclaves that promise to find our reason for us" (1941; p. 43). Existence is perceived by individuals lacking matured critical thinking skills as "essentially chaotic, with no meaning or rationality" (Brookfield, 1987, p. 43). In brief, the main problem is in a world lacking pre-emptive critical thinking, is a world pervaded by endless challenges, crises, and issues lacking a feasible solution, as well as the possibility for averting the conundrum.

The Three Core Aims:

The first aim of engaging therein the unbridled pursuit of advanced critical thinking is the aiding and helping of administrators, faculty, and target students, to understand the phenomenon of critical thinking. This phenomenon awareness (herein referenced as PA) entails describing the essential components, providing examples of how it can be observed in people's actions, and setting out the research and conceptual base for this 15 activity (Brookfield, 1987, p. x). The second aim; it entails the thorough examination of various methods, techniques, and approaches that can be used by anyone aspiring to help people develop better critical thinking skills. This provides various case studies of successful practice and outlines specific exercises designed to foster critical thinking (Brookfield, 1987, p. x). The third aim; it entails the thorough exploration of diverse opportunities for people becoming advanced critical thinkers, in *four key arenas*: 1. Intimate relationships; 2. Workplace; 3. Political involvements, and; 4. Mass media, all acutely germane to its influence upon the perception of reality (Brookfield, 1987, p. x).

The Foundational Pillars of Quantum Acad(yna^{E3})mics^{SM®}:

This dissertation-proposal—blueprint schematics, is constructed, drafted, and established upon the following five foundational pillars. Firstly, the circumference-pillars include: 1. Pillar one—Analysis of concepts correlating to intuitive knowing, thinking, and understanding; 2. Pillar two—Analysis of concepts pertinent to perception and its core tenets; 3. Pillar three—Research applicable to similar, inter-related studies; 4. Pillar four—Drafting of link between information collected and real-world application [See Appendix 'A', for Figure 1]. Lastly, the central pillar is that mankind is comprised of three basic aspects, aka the "Trinity of mankind": 1. The Soma; 2. The Psuche'; 3. The Pneuma ("The Therapon Trichotomy Model", 2009). The Soma, aka the "Body of Man" is the physical, impirical, and sensual system. The Psuche, aka the "Mind of Man", is comprised of the mind, body, and the emotional system. The Pneuma, aka the "Supernatural Essence of Man", is the realm in which a SF, phenomenon, or higher power (God or Creator) dwell, lives, and occupies therein [See Appendix 'B', for Figure 2].

Supplemental-Philosophical Background:

The author's encompassing life mantra (herein referenced as LM)—theory in action, or the "theory of deliberate human behavior" is that existing at the deepest core of all learners-students is the limitless potential for manifesting total transformation, literally at all levels simultaneously (Argyris, and Schön, 1974, p. 6). In other words, for every 1 situation S, if consequence C is desired, then the applicable party ought to engage in activity 'A' [See Appendix 'C', for Figure 3]. There is a seed of change, development, and growth lying dormant, waiting to be identified, as well as awakened, stimulated, and quickened. It is best defined, thus summarized as quantum—quasi-dimensional, metamorphosis, all of which has yet to be tapped into, unleashed, and fully realized. Only after this next-level transformation has first occurred intrinsically can anyone begin to likewise effectuate constructive and lasting change into their corresponding spheres of influence—locally, regionally, and globally.

The chief premise for this aspect of the proposed—Quantum Acad(yna^{E3})mics$^{SM®}$ Theoretical Learning Framework (herein referenced as TLF)—system, is that TLF is the undisputed responsibility of administrators, educators, faculty, and the similar to prepare the next-generation of students—leaders, problem solvers, and thinkers. TLF is a system, where educators ought to "want them to help us form an institution that can respond to demands of a future that we cannot yet see very clearly" (Maxwell, 2009, p. 7). In brief, the target body of student-learners predictably becomes competent and effective socio-change agents within their corresponding spheres of influence—locally, regionally, and globally.

Research Problem in the Context of the Theoretical Framework:

The encompassing problem and overall intent of this study involves the 5 unprecedented and out-of-control crises occurring within the context of the American educational system, plus the encompassing world at-large. Concerning higher education—for example, firstly there is a rising concern that in an age earmarked by astounding technological breakthroughs, a vast majority of educators are witnessing a swift exodus away from the vital human element. Sandler (2012) reports that many young students characterize the academic-setting as an impersonal place where faculty did not have enough time, and was lackadaisical in understanding plus having respect for their backgrounds and communities (p. 20). Germane to the world at-large; for example, lastly there is the increasing sense of urgency in finding alternative sources of energy and fuel. Cremer and Weitzman (2002) assert that the Organization of the Petroleum Exporting Countries is essentially "viewed as a monopolist sharing the oil market with a competitive sector". Nonetheless, the comprehensive problem has become an epidemic of such historic proportions, that if a soundly developed solution plan is not straightway developed, America's ability to resurrect her posture as an iconic-example of technological superiority will become a hapless-capitulation. The problem; firstly, includes the lack of facilitating group consensus-driven academic learning that is wholly servant-natured driven plus focused, and secondly, the undervaluing and oversight of having a sense of urgency in engineering a pre-emptive strategic system of critical learning, thinking, and understanding, that is fundamentally transformational and transactional, plus most importantly intuitive and predictive. In other words, the proposed system is essentially a balanced system of comprehensive analytics, insofar that the insights and opinions of each constituent or team-member—ranging from least-preferred to most-preferred, is indiscriminately weighed and thus considered for active utilization. In brief, it consistently involves the integration of a pre-emptive system that is highly intuitive and predicatively anticipatory. As a direct result thereof, the possibility for effectively addressing and responding to diverse crises or social conundrums will not only be significantly enhanced, but possibly averted at the point-of-inception. Thus, this can literally mean the preservation and protection of the corresponding economy—correlating to tens-of-millions, up to and including hundreds-of-billions of dollars, as well as mutual trust, peace and collective solidarity of relevant constituents. And such, is the crux—heart or pulse, of this focused research study-proposal.

Formulation of the Research Questions, Hypotheses, and Purpose of the Study

[Research Questions (RQ)]

Quantitative Research Questions:

- ⅄ Is there substantive evidence to confirm or disconfirm that intuition and predictive analysis play a significant part in the enhancement of advanced critical thinking?
- ⅄ Is there substantive evidence to corroborate and validate that there is a great price plus significant value in pain, as well as suffering?

Qualitative Research Questions:

- ⅄ Is it possible to have reflection and intuition as complementary processes, within the context of an organization?
- ⅄ Does the integration of intuition and predictive analysis into the critical thinking process, contribute, add value, and increase the overall efficacy to the resulting quality thereof?

Purpose of the Study:

The target and specific purpose for this—mixed methods research—study is to assess and determine if the integration, plus the reinforcement with a system of pre-emptive—intuitive and predictive—critical thinking-analytics will increase and enhance the overall efficacy of already implemented solution plans. This will be achieved via the ongoing engagement of investigative-research, and the facilitation of diverse assessment instruments—qualitative and quantitative. In brief, this endeavor will consequentially affirm, as well as prove that there is a direct correlation between the integration of the Quantum Acad(yna^{E3})mics$^{SM®}$ Strategic System into already implemented, conventional solution plans; it will also include the significant increase of overall efficacy. Thus, the hypotheses—primary hypothesis and secondary hypothesis—will be confirmed and thus proven as credible, feasible, reliable, trustworthy, and valid.

Hypotheses:

The dissertation-proposal hypotheses concentrate upon the reinforcement of conventional critical thinking (herein referenced as CT) plans, with a CT-system that is intuitive and anticipatory. The primary hypothesis proposes that the skillful integration of the proposed strategic—blueprint-schematics, system into already implemented and conventional solution plans, results in both enhancement and increase of overall efficacy. The secondary hypothesis proposes that the collected data confirms and reinforces the necessities for fusing together intuitive abilities, aptitudes, and practices in the integration of conventional systems of critical thinking.

Null Hypothesis:

The null hypothesis confirms and demonstrates that if intuition and predictive—analytics are not integrated into conventional solution plans, no change in overall efficacy results, one way or the other. Thus, there is no need for having a sense of urgency for integrating intuition or predictive-analytics into conventional solution plans; in the final analysis, no precautionary measures are deemed necessary.

Review of Literature

[Foundational Worldview & Theoretical Frameworks]

Social Constructivist Worldview (SCW):

This philosophical worldview of SCW; social constructivist worldview was originally developed and first proposed by Lev Vygotsky. He is considered as an idealistic Anti-Communist. His theoretical worldview concentrates a vast majority of energy and time, plus diverse other critical resources towards the group consensus-nature of both education and learning. Kim citing Derry & McMahon (2012) affirms and thus emphasizes the importance of culture and context in understanding what occurs in society and constructing knowledge based on this understanding (1999; 1997, ¶1). It is, in fact, a consolidation of several cognitive constructivist models. Nonetheless, pertinent to the core context of this mock dissertation proposal, it "argues that all cognitive functions originate in, and must therefore be explained as products of social interactions and that learning was not simply the assimilation and accommodation of new knowledge by learners; it was the process by which learners were integrated into a knowledge community" (Vygotsky, 1978, ¶1). In brief, the underlying notion is that all activities involving advanced critical thinking—plus cognitive-driven debate and discourse, is influenced by many dynamic factors of fluctuating variability—hidden or overt. All of which directly connects and correlates to the contextual specificities of the encompassing community. However, germane to the subtle, yet obvious research-void, there is no mention of the concepts of intuition or predictive-analysis. Thus, the major issue or primary question which remains grossly unanswered is; how might the development of group consensus, and the construction of vital knowledge, be greatly enhanced with value plus overall efficacy, if intuition and predictive analytics were fully integrated?

Transformational Leadership Theory (TLT):

The underlying premise of TLT is that leadership education and training exists for the sole purpose of affording and facilitating such a level of high-quality academics, all of which consequentially results in the lasting and ongoing constructive change, growth, and development of its corresponding student body of learners. In other words, the most common, plus prevalent characteristics, plus traits is that "such leaders are visionary, inspiring, daring, risk-takers, and thoughtful thinkers. They have a charismatic appeal" ("Management Study Guide", 2008-2012, ¶1). Bass (2002-2012) notes that transformational leadership which is acutely authentic—is grounded in moral foundations based upon four critical or vital components; these components are idealized influence, inspirational motivation, intellectual stimulation, and individualized consideration" ("Changingminds.com", ¶3).

Moreover, Bass (2002-2012) asserts that authentic transformational leadership is also comprised of the moral character of the leader, the ethical values embedded in the leader's vision, articulation, and program (which followers either embrace or reject), and lastly the morality of the processes of social ethical choice and action that leaders and followers engage in and collectively pursue (¶3). In brief, if a prospective leader possesses each one of the listed components, they can expect to become a leader whom is wholly transformational [See Appendix 'D', for Figure 4].

However, germane to the subtle, yet obvious research-void, there is, again, the failure in acknowledging or mentioning the concepts of intuition and predictive-analysis. The major question remaining unanswered is; how might the development of leaders be greatly enhanced if the concepts of intuition and predictive analysis were integrated? These exceptional leaders possess the following attributes: 1. great visionaries; 2. Inspiring; 3. courageous plus daring; 4. risk-takers, and; 5. highly analytical and reflective thinkers, all whom possess elements of true charismatic appeal.

Contingency Leadership Theory (CLT):

The underlying premise of CLT is that if any organization aspires to achieve a level of highly effective group leadership, the organization must first and foremost ensure that it thoroughly assesses the corresponding leadership candidate, in accordance to an encompassing, the specific situation confronting him or her, and thus establish a correlating match thereof. In other words, the employing company needs to "assess the leader according to an underlying trait, assess the situation faced by the leader, and construct a proper match between the two" ("Management Study Guide Online", 2008-25 2012, ¶1).

Furthermore, Fielder (2008-2012) reveals that in order to rightly assess the attitudes of the leader, it is imperative to identify and thus actively take into consideration the team member considered as the least preferred co-worker (LPC) ("Management Study Guide Online", 2008-2012, ¶1). Hence, the LPC scale is a questionnaire "in which the leaders are asked about the person with whom they least like to work"; it consists of "items used to reflect a leader's underlying disposition toward others" ("Management Study Online", 2008-2012, ¶1). In brief, the overarching objective is the complete and total concentrated upon the distinct correlation between the recognized body of leadership, and the overall performance of the collective organization [See Appendix E', for Table 1]. However, germane to the subtle, yet obvious gap-in-research, there is no evidence of the concepts of intuition or predictive analysis being referred to. In fact, in the process of thoroughly assessing prospective leadership candidates, it is surprising that the evidence of intuitive propensity or accuracy in predictive anticipation is not even considered as part of the equation. In brief, the distinct research-gap involves the author's lack of consideration pertinent to how valuable intuition and predictive analysis weighs in measuring how able and competent prospective leaders are in handing diverse crisis which arise in their corresponding situational contexts.

Servant Leadership Theory (SLT):

The underlying premise of SLT; it is that the posture of occupying a position of leadership is to serve other individuals, particularly one's team of followers to whom one is appointed to lead. It was first developed and proposed by Robert Greenleaf. Waddell citing Greenleaf (2006) asserts that—the servant-leader is servant first, which begins with the natural feeling that one wants to serve. Following the desire to serve may be a conscious choice that brings one to aspire to lead. The leader-first and the servant-first are two extreme types of leaders with the servant-first leader taking care to make sure other people's highest priority needs are being served. (1991; p. 2).

The key idea, anyhow, is that the leader's primary reason for existence is to assertively and eagerly invest all of the necessary resources—energy, time, and etcetera—which ultimately results in the follower becoming wholly matured—changed, developed, and thus grown in to a higher dimension of overall effectiveness. Waddell citing Patterson's dissertation (2006) concedes that the theory of servant leadership is but a logical extension of transformational leadership theory. Thus, she also defines and develops the component constructs underlying the practice of servant leadership; servant leaders are essentially defined as those leaders who lead an organization by focusing on their followers, such that the followers are the primary concern and the organizational concerns are (2003, p. 5; p. 2). In brief, if a leader is to be considered, thus defined as a servant leader, that one must assertively endeavor to place the needs of one's follower(s) far above the needs of oneself [See Appendix 'F', for Figure 5].

However, germane to the subtle, yet obvious gap-in-research, there is no evidence of the concepts of intuition or predictive analysis being referred to. In other words, the overarching idea is that the primary responsibility of the leader is to ensure that each follower is afforded the maximum amount to energy, time, and other critical resources towards their full maturation process. It is here that the research-gap is fully revealed and exposed. And such, yields the question; how much more effective would leaders be in facilitating the requisite knowledge plus experience unto their followers, if elements of intuition and predictive analysis were considered a vital part of the comprehensive process? In brief, if leaders were equipped and trained in utilizing intuition plus predictive-analytics, they would be that much more effective plus efficient in preparing their designated team of followers. Thus, energy, time, and vital other resources would be significantly preserved and reduced.

Transactional Leadership Theory (TLT):

The underlying premise of TLT is that leadership is a process of ongoing and continuous exchange. Leadership is a process involving the leader—himself or herself—as well as the leader and one's delegated team of followers, or subordinates. TLT is such a leadership model which has developed and been thus revised several times, within the past few decades. For example, Bass and Weber (2010-2012) divulge that "Punishment and reward motivate people and this underpins transactional leadership theories" (p. ¶3). Also, this theoretical model asserts that a clear and irrefutable leadership chain-of-command must be both identified and recognized. Bass and Weber (2010-2012) confess that, "there must be a well-defined hierarchy, where everyone knows who the leader is and who is following" (¶3). After all, when vast individuals are in harmonic agreement, pertinent to the needs of the organization, and completing a set array of goals and objectives, any possibility for conflict-internal strife will be averted. In brief, main idea is that if any organization or team is to be successful, there ought to exist, both the willingness to compromise and thus work harmonically together. As well as the full understanding as to who is delegated within the ranks of leadership, versus those identified within the rank-and-file of subordinates.

However, germane to the subtle, yet obvious research-void, the author did not make any reference to the applicability plus relevance of intuition and predictive analysis into the initial equation. In other words, when the necessity for either punishment or reward is deemed essential, the lack of consideration for intuition and predictive analytics can grossly compromise or even undermine to overall rate of accuracy in determining which one ought to be facilitated over the other. In brief, if intuition and predictive analysis, conversely, were considered as having a weight of priority, the ability to determine and thus pre-emptive response to corresponding situations, both could and would be significantly increased, as well as greatly enhanced germane to overall efficacy; and so, does this investigative analysis now official commences!

Literature Review Plan for the Dissertation Proposal:

This dissertation-proposal commences with first addressing and critiquing the overarching problem—challenges, issues, and crisis, pervading and permeating America's educational system, as well as the world at-large. Secondly, the researcher then actively engages in investigative research pertinent to diverse frameworks and theories essential and relevant towards the engineering of a comprehensive strategic system—*blueprint-schematics*, which is pre-emptive in nature. In brief, this plan also proposes and defends the notion that the aforementioned crises can not only be addressed and responded to in a most expedient manner, but most importantly reverses and perhaps even averts the impending conundrum in the first place. Thus, this proposal and active line of defense is achieved via the acquisition and analytical assessment of the seceding peer-reviewed plus research-driven articles.

[Relevant and Pertinent Research Articles]

Prediction Errors and Attention in the Presence and Absence of Feedback:

The overarching principle is that individuals invest more energy, time, and personal resources towards to research and study of material for which they have limited knowledge and understanding. Wills (2009) asserts that "We appear to learn more about things for which we initially make incorrect predictions than we do about things for which our initial predictions are correct" (p. 95). In brief, the main and final interpretation is that scientific research confirms that the human brain has an increased predilection towards concentrate greater attention and focus towards those otherwise gray areas of the world in which prediction has proven either in error, invalid, or grossly insufficient.

Quality of Electronic Services—Conceptualizing and Testing a Hierarchical Model:

The overarching principle is that automated and electronic technology is given increased attention and active utilization in the realm of academics. Fassnacht and Koese (2012) confirms that over the long haul—appropriate conceptualization and measurement are crucial for an effective management of service quality, particularly on the Internet (p. 15 33). The overall delivery and facilitation of high service quality, in turn, is necessary for customer satisfaction and loyalty in the online world (Fassnacht and Koese, 2012, p. 33). In brief, the chief advantage of utilizing technology in the sphere of academics is that it has real world and pragmatic application in our current digital era.

Intuition—Myth or a Decision-making Tool:

The overarching principle is that intuition is far more than a superstitious belief. Ashkanasy and Sinclair citing Epstein et al. (2012) confer that intuition is a "non-sequential information processing mode, which comprises both cognitive and affective elements and results in direct knowing without any use of conscious reasoning" (p. 357). Furthermore, it could be considered similar to—a non-conscious scanning of internal (in memory) and external (in environment) resources in a non-logical, non-temporal manner in order to identify relevant pieces of information that are fitted into the "solution picture in a seemingly haphazard way" (Ashkanasy and Sinclair, 2012, p. p. 357). 30 15

In brief, the end result is that there undeniably exist both advantages and disadvantages in utilizing such an often intangible ability, which otherwise cannot always be calculated and monitored utilizing scientific methods. Thus, an accurate measurement of intuitive decision making remains a challenge (Ashkanasy and Sinclair, 2012, p. 365). Supplemental investigative research is required.

The Price of Pain and the Value of Suffering:

The overarching principle is that when confronted with the evidence of pain, overall people are willing to pay more to avoid pain as it is intensified. In fact, pertinent to quantitative statistical research the "price offers for relief of medium pain were higher when the pain was experienced in a sequence including many low-pain trials (low-medium block), compared with when the same pain was experienced in a sequence including many high-pain trials (medium-high block)" (Chater et al., 2009, p. 312). In brief, the chief advantage of pain and suffering is that is can serve as a reliable catalyst for intense motivation, whenever when it is deemed essential and thus considered necessary.

Teaching Style and Learning in a Quantitative Classroom:

The overarching principle is that there are direct benefits, as well as neutral or no positive results for integrating inquiry-based classes along with the active fusion of learning and diverse teaching styles. In other words, the most important predicting factor is the specific situational factors prevalent at the time in which the aforementioned factors are facilitated. In other words, pertinent to the comparative analysis involving teacher-centered techniques, comprehensive critical analysis, integration of intuition and predictive-analytics, along with student-centered technique, the final analysis is "in general, the teacher-centered approach appeared to give students a slight advantage over students in the student-centered class" (p. 220). In brief, the final result only corroborates the notion that education, in most cases, which places greater weight towards the teacher's needs being met, as opposed to the student's needs, maximum productivity and positive results occurs with greater prevalence.

The Organization in Balance—Reflection and Intuition as Complementary Processes:

The overarching principle is that if reflection and intuition are carefully facilitated, simultaneously, there is increased likelihood and probability for the manifestation of balance—peace, and synergistic-tranquility. Korthagen (2005) mentions that the main or operative question involves; how can we see to it that people are willing and able to adjust to constantly changing circumstances (p. 371). Kothagen citing Mintzberg (2005) reveals—the model of core reflection seems to be helpful in supporting this integration of reflection and intuiting in professional (1976; p. 384). Thus, the main idea is that the careful and systematic integration of intuition with reflection "can create real change in culture compared with the more common tendency to focus on rational analysis"; it fosters and results in a safe plus secured, as well as highly stimulating work environment, and a culture in which failures are accepted and embraced as a necessary element or component of learning (Kothagen emphasizing Argyris, 1993; 2005, p. 384). In brief, learning will be highly maximized with long-term beneficial results.

The Role of Intuition in Collective Learning and the Development of Shared Meaning:

The overarching principle is that the facilitation and utilization of intuitive abilities greatly enhances and thus increases the overall positive experience in group contextual learning, shared knowledge interpretation, and a deep understanding. Sadler-Smith (2008) asserts that, intuitive judgments based on nonconscious pattern recognition and somatic state activation/awareness is acknowledged as significant in human decision-making processes (p. 494). In other words, germane to the context of managerial or leadership-based cognition, the active utilization of intuition "is one of the principle means by which leadership or management makes complex decisions, particularly in loosely structured environments" (Sadler-Smith citing Burke and Miller at al., 1999; 25 2008, p. 494). In brief, the main idea is that management most essentially use gut feeling discretion in determining whether the utilization of intuition is considered either feasible, or necessary.

Research Design and Methodology:

The mixed methods research study is an integration of the qualitative and quantitative research methods (Creswell, 2009, p. 4). It assesses and determines the resulting effects of reinforcing or integrating intuition and predictive-analytics into conventional solution plans. It determines if the overall efficacy of conventional solution plans will be greatly enhanced—evidence of significant direct correlation, and thus improves as a direct result. In other words, the final analysis will confirm or disconfirm; affirm or refute the credibility, reliability, trustworthiness, and overall validity of the proposed advanced—Quantum Acad(yna^{E3})mics$^{SM®}$—strategic, critical thinking system. Also, it is fundamentally comprised of three core phases. However, for the sake of observing the applicable constraints and limitations, pertinent to the overall depth breadth, and length of this brief proposal, only phase one will be addressed and discussed. Therein the full context of the official dissertation—if considered and deemed acceptable by the esteemed committee, will phase two, and phase three be discussed.

Quantitative Design and Methodology:

The quantitative design method; it is interpreted and understood as a practice in which the attainment of empirical evidence is considered of the utmost importance. This design method is commonly identified through the facilitation and utilization of two common strategies. The first is experimental designs or quasi-experiments. The second is non-experimental designs or research surveys. However, only the research survey will be officially utilized within the context of this dissertation-proposal. In direct response to the question, what is a survey research; Creswell asserts that "it provides a quantitative or numeric description of trends, attitudes, or opinions of a population by studying a sample of that population" (2009, p. 12). In brief, the ultimate objective is the identification of common patterns existing throughout the target sample-market.

Phase One:

Phase one; it essentially involves the facilitation of the "SurveyMonkey" (SurveyMonkey.com), "a commercial product available since 1999" (Creswell, 2009, p. 148). It is a single-staged sampling procedure that will be administered—online—to adult-level students, as well as other individuals from a pre-selected sample-audience, all who will consequentially respond to a quantitative-based assessment survey. This survey acquires statistical-empirical evidence that will further assess and determine the overall reliability and validity of the total study. In other words, once the data has been officially collected, generated, and hence measured—as descriptive statistics, it will then be printed in report form. This report will then be utilized in phases two and three—in the official dissertation study—applicable towards the thorough completion of the breadth and length of the collective research study. In brief, the chief purpose for the facilitation of the quantitative instrument is to assess, confirm, and likewise verify both reliability and validity.

Validity of Results:

Validity of results involves "whether one can draw meaningful and useful inferences from scores on the instruments" (Creswell, 2009, p. 149). Concerning the actual type of validity that it serves to validate, there are two: 1. Predictive validity; 2. Construct validity. Predictive validity, firstly; it checks for the correlation between the resulting or tabulated score, and the target criterion in which it was intended. Construct validity, secondly, rather checks for distinct correlation between the specific items measured, and the hypothetical concepts or constructs in which it applies.

Reliability of Results:

Reliability of results involves the assessment as to whether scores-data resulting from past use of the instrument fully corroborates with that which has been initially predicted (Creswell, 2009, p. 149). Thus, the main objective is to thoroughly investigate whether or not the collected results are consistent across constructs, as well as the same results being considered consistent, and stable over a predetermined period of time; specifically after administration of the identical assessment, the second time around (Creswell, 2009, p. 150). Another important issue that will be assessed and weighed is whether or not the evidence of errors is a direct result of gross negligence or the indifference of either the corresponding team of administrators, or perhaps the designated results-keepers.

Qualitative Design and Methodology:

The qualitative design method is considered and recognized as a means for exploring and understanding the specific meaning designated by persons—individually and collectively. It intends to ascribe or define a problem that is either human in-nature, or social in-nature. This design method is typically identified through the facilitation and utilization of two common strategies. The first is case studies. The second is phenomenological research. However, only the phenomenological research method will be utilized throughout the length of this brief dissertation-proposal. The phenomenological research method is an investigative process where researchers "review their data as they are collected and record and write up their hunches, initial analyses, and questions in the form of research memos" (Lodico et al., 2010, p. 180). It is fundamentally an inductive process that seeks to verify both quality and relevancy in its pragmatic application.

Pertinent to its application within the context of this research study, questionnaires, as well as both interview sessions and observational settings will occur, of course in each participants 'natural sphere of influence. It is facilitated with an inductive approach where the desired and required patterns of behavior, target responses, and underlying themes are developed as a direct result of the actual data collected. However, the actual instrument facilitated to each distinct target or sample-audience is hence modified or calibrated in such a way that the corresponding holistic-theoretical lens—influences the results one way or the other, is actively considered then engaged. The main objective is that identification of common patterns existing throughout the target sample-market. In brief, this method involves the: 1. Facilitation of key or pertinent questionnaires, as well as; 2. Scheduling of interview-sessions. Questionnaires will be forwarded to hand-selected individuals, within the context of the participant's environmental setting; it includes place of employment, various conferences in which one attends, scheduled lectures, or even symposiums of interest. Data will also be collected via the scheduling of interview-sessions for designated team-members to meet, plus observe the pre-identified sample-audience. In brief, once the interview has been completely established, the candidate will then report to a pre-determined location, and meet with the appointed interview team or staff.

Disclaimer Notice:

The sample-audience, in which each of the preceding assessment instruments will be facilitated, is as follows: 1. Age; 2. Gender; 3. Ethnicity; 4. Education.

Firstly, the age range is adults between the ages of 18 and 55; this the specific age range in which individuals are endeavoring to extend and continue in his or her career. This involves those returning to school for additional education and training, or even relevance certification courses, specialization, and training. Secondly, the study involves participants who are—genderal specification, both male and females. Next, the cultural-ethnicity of the participants is as follows: 1. Anglo-Saxon; 2. Afro-American; 3. Hispanic-American; 4. Latin-American; 5. Spanish-American; 6. Asian-Americans; 7. Eastern Indian-American; 8. Middle Eastern. Lastly, the educational background includes individuals with no more than Graduate Equivalency Diploma (GED), up to and including Graduate Degree holders. Hence, the main reason for this decision is that the preceding categories comprise the greatest percentage of citizens residing with the boundaries of the Continental-United States. In brief, it endeavors to identify the overall pulse or voice of the collective American people, at-large.

Sources of Data Collection and Data Analysis:

The target sample-audience comprises adult-level learners, plus administration and faculty. This essentially includes diverse professionals from the disciplines of counseling and psychology; the social sciences, atmospheric and environmental sciences; the military, and individuals employed with the fields of science and technology. The team of assessment facilitators includes professionals from the fields of counseling, education, mathematics—experts in computations, permutations, predictions, 25 probability, and descriptive statistics, and information sciences, plus information technology. Research assistants will also be available to address and respond to question which might arise from participants. These individuals are also available to provide any type of assistance to the same participants. The underlying purpose for this is to provide maximum time for team of professionals and specialist to address, and respond to key elements, all requisite in ensuring that the overall experience is of the highest level of standards plus excellence. Once the participants arrive, the first activity involves the signing of the official guest-visitation roster sheet. The specific information collected includes: 1. Name; 2. Physical address; 3. Contact number; 4. Field of expertise; 5. Email. In brief, this ensures that not only each participant is not only accounted for, but also to receive the official final report.

The next step in the process is a brief session in which instructions are provided. Once this process is completed, participants are then provided a five-minute break, in order to prepare himself or herself for matriculating throughout the entire length of process. After returning from the five-minute intermission, an informed consent form is provided—reviewed, signed, and returned. Next, data collection forms and questionnaires are administered. The total time required for the interview, plus information gathering session is one-hour and fifteen minutes; the first twenty-five minutes is focused towards the completion of the questionnaire—includes 50 total questions—plus background analysis form-profile. The remaining fifty minutes is afforded towards the completion of the interview. This includes the facilitation of a series of questions, analysis of patterns, and a most inflective and reflective study that is wholly predictive. The main objective is to assess the individuals: 1. Experience with intuition and predictive analysis; 2. Analysis of historical issues and crises; 3. Input concerning personal-professional insights and recommendations; 4. Tests—aptitude and skills which measures the participants' ability. While this activity is occurring, it is noted that data will be gathered via audio recording of session, and video recorded. This entire process in held with the highest-level of strictest confidence; it will not be sold or shared with individuals outside of the Quantum Acad(yna^{E3})mics$^{SM®}$ Strategic System Network. It is fully completed and facilitated through the active partnership with a private research gathering firm such as Fieldwork, Inc.—Consumer Market and Research Firm. The direct contact number, as listed in the Dallas Yellow Pages Business Directory, is 972/866-5820. Pertinent to the nominal compensation-fees given for time invested, each participant is provided $150, in the form of a check that can be deposited or cashed at their personal banking facility. Lastly, the desired analysis of collected data will be achieved through the active utilization of the Statistical Package for the Social Sciences Software Package.

Considering that the comprehensive study is of the descriptive nature, the data method that will be the focus is what is called numerical statistics. Note, descriptive statistics is the brand of statistics which measures numerical data that assess and analyzes phenomena, or as in the case of this study it will measure human and social phenomena. The overarching tasks of the researcher is to describe sets or patterns of information, and hence make accurate inferences about applicable or target groups based upon the complete and incomplete gaps of information. Thus, the data will be: 1. Gathered; 2. Organized; 3. Analyzed plus assessed.

The ultimate goal and objective is to make accurate inferences, which results from the processing and analysis of the information collected. The types of formula or concepts that will be actively considered and utilized—quantitative frame-of-reference, is the determination of the measures of central tendency and measures of variability. It will also include the utilization of Linear Correlation Coefficient Studies, as well as Confidence Intervals. Ruffo divulges that—measures of central tendency are numbers which tend to clutter around the middle of a set of values (1993, p. 27). The objective is to assess and determine the mean, median, and the mode of the collected data. Ruffo (1993) also reveals that the measures of variation intend to determine the range, and the deviation plus variance of the data, as well as the standard deviation of the results thereof. A range is defined as "the difference between the largest and smallest values" (Ruffo, 1993, p. 35). The deviation is defined as "the distance of the measurements away from the mean" (Ruffo, 1993, p. 34). The variance is defined as "the sum of the squared deviations of n measurements from their mean divided by (n-1)" (Ruffo, 1993, p. 34). The standard deviation is defined as—the positive square root of the variance (Ruffo, 1993, p. 35). Lastly, Triola (2007) asserts that the basic notion of measuring linear correlation of coefficients is to determine the "strength of the relationship between two variables representing quantitative data" (p. 547). In sum, the primary reason for considering the SPSS software is because it is recognized and regarded as a most reliable mode of technology to engage therein the necessary statistical and predictive analyses, for arriving at the most accurate and correct results.

Potential and Anticipated Results:

The potential and anticipated result of this comprehensive study is that substantive information will be gathered. If fact, if a direct correlation is irrefutably proven and thus confirmed, then the collective dissertation-proposal hypotheses will be affirmed and confirmed. The primary hypothesis; the skillful integration of the proposed strategic—blueprint schematics, system into already implemented conventional solution plans, will result in both enhanced and increased overall efficacy. Likewise, the secondary hypothesis will be affirmed and fully confirmed. The collected data will defend the proposed posture, asserting the fusion of intuitive abilities, aptitudes, and practices with conventional methods-systems of critical thinking will be increased and enhanced germane to overall efficacy. Conversely, the null hypothesis will be fully disproven and refuted; that there is no direct correlation between increased intuition and conventional critical thinking, plus its urgent necessity for integrating into traditional solution plans and consequentially engage therein the necessary precautionary measures. This null hypothesis is fully and irrefutably disproven. In brief, the collective ad comprehensive study will confirm and validate that if the proposed—blueprint-schematics—Quantum Acad(yna^{E3})mics^{SM} Strategic System is skillfully fused together in the reinforcement of conventional critical thinking solution plans, a vast majority of crises will be wholly avoided, reversed, or perhaps even wholly averted.

Conclusion:

In conclusion, the encompassing problem and overall intent of this study involves the unprecedented and out-of-control crisis occurring within the context of the American educational system, plus the world at-large. The comprehensive problem has become an epidemic of such historic proportions, that if a soundly developed solution plan is not straightway developed, America's ability to resurrect her posture as an iconic-example of technological superiority will become a hapless-capitulation.

Regarding the theoretical learning frameworks considered acutely and germane to the foundational underpinnings of the comprehensive proposal, they include:

1. Transformational Leader Theory;
2. Contingency Leadership Theory;
3. Servant Leadership Theory;
4. Transactional Leadership Theory.

The target and specific purpose for this—mixed methods research—study is to assess and determine if the integration, plus the reinforcement with a system of pre-emptive—intuitive and predictive—critical thinking-analytics will increase and enhance the overall efficacy of conventional, and already implemented solution plans. From the quantitative frame-of-reference, a survey research assessment is utilized. The chief purpose for utilizing such as instrument is the identification of common patterns existing throughout the target sample-market. From a qualitative frame-of-reference, a phenomenological research assessment will be facilitated. The chief purpose for the utilization of this instrument is because it is will verify the both quality and overall relevancy of the data-information that is collected and gathered. Pertinent to its application, questionnaires, as well as both interview sessions and observational settings will occur, all within the context of the participants'natural sphere of influence. In brief, the potential and anticipated results will only confirm and irrefutably affirm that there does exist credibility, reliability, trustworthiness, and overall validity within the encompassing context of the proposed advanced—Quantum Acad(yna^{E3})mics$^{SM®}$—strategic, critical thinking system.

The Quantum—Idea, Concept?:

Underlying Inspiration of Quantum Acad(yna^{E3})mics$^{SM®}$

The principle upon which the comprehensive framework of The Quantum Acad(yna^{E3}) mics$^{SM®}$ Strategic System is established, was first developed, engineered, and proposed by Professor, and distinguished plus notable scientists Niels Bohr, Max Planck—*Father of the Quantum Theory*, and Albert Einstein—*Father of the Theory of Relativity*. It was first officially presented to the scientific community in the early part of the 20th Century. In brief, the official name of this astounding and world-transforming theory is the "Quantum Theory of Light".

This novel and breakthrough theory, in fact, arose "out of the need to reconcile the wavelike behavior of light with its particle-like behavior" (Taffel, 1986, p. 311). In essence, the rudimentary tenets of this theory asserts "light is emitted from luminous bodies in tiny packets of energy called photon" or quanta (Taffel, 1986, p. 313). In brief, the chief premise is that each photon or quanta—packets or bundles of energy, "is associated with light waves of a specific frequency" . . . "it has a fixed, definite quantity of energy proportional to that frequency" (Taffel, 1986, p. 311).

Epilogue:

The world in which we live is swiftly changing right before our very eyes. Just within the past decade, there has been intensifying national debate pertaining to America's dire need for ending its dependence upon fuel reserves derived from "oil-gas producing" Middle Eastern countries. The chief international conglomerate which facilitates the distribution of these reserves is commonly referred to as the Organization of the Petroleum Exporting Countries (OPEC). OPEC was first developed in 1960-15 Baghdad, Iraq, with its main function serving to—regulate oil production, and thereby manages oil prices, in a coordinated effort among the member countries ("OPEC", 2004). It is essentially "viewed as a monopolist sharing the oil market with a competitive sector" (Cremer & Weitzman, 2002). OPEC is thus comprised of the following core nations: 1. Algeria; 2. Indonesia; 3. Iran; 4. Iraq; 5. Kuwait,; 6. Libya; 7. Nigeria; 8. Qatar; 9. Saudi 20 Arabia; 10. United Arab Emirates; 11. Venezuela ("OPEC", 2004).

Existing at the nucleus of this ongoing debate is the need to design, develop, and implement alternative methods for which this endeavor can become a reality. It will require the active and unwavering commitment of its leaders and delegated powers-that-be to engage into a series of much needed—think tank-driven sessions. A prime example of the type of discourse that will contribute greatly towards the overall outcome is the "Appreciative Inquiry (AI) Model". AI; it is defined as a group process that inquires into, identifies, and further develops the best of what is "in organizations in order to create a better future" (Preskill & Catsambas, 2006, p. 1). Moreover, it—helps align evaluation activities with an organization's mission and performance goals 30 (Preskill & Catsambas, 2006, p. 99). It consists of two fundamental components: 1. "4-D Model"; 2. "4-I Model". Also, the 4-D consists of four phases: 1. Discovering; 2. Dreaming; 3. Designing; 4. Destiny. Likewise, the 4-I consists of four phases: 1. Inquire; 2. Imagine; 3. Innovate; 4. Implement (Preskill, 2006, p. 8, slides 15-16). In short, AI affords the relevant decision making parties the requisite particulars for ensuring that the required energy, resources, and time invested produces, in the end, quantified-dividends.

Nevertheless, pertinent to the underlying thread which runs throughout the length and breadth of this course project, it requires that two fundamentally core components exist: 1. Innovation, and; 2. Execution. The main reason as to why innovation and execution are considered essential components, plus core elements is because they are considered as the chief pillars upon which the comprehensive critical thinking (CT) system irrefutably exists thereon. That is, in order for the totality of CT to materialize—start to finish, creative innovation must immediately (double-underscored) be followed by unfaltering and unprecedented action-execution. Brookfield (1987) echoes this sentiment with affirming that—We have seen that critical thinking comprises two interrelated processes: identifying and challenging assumptions, and imagining and exploring alternatives (p. 229). Innovation that is not followed with immediate execution often results in utter-total failure.

According to The New International Webster's Standard Dictionary (2006) innovation is defined as "n. something new; the process of introducing something new" (p. 151). Execution, on the other hand is understood as the necessary steps that an entity—individual, organizational, or otherwise, must effectuate or engage therein so that the desired results will consequentially result. It is defined as—n. 1. The state or process of acting or doing; 2. A movement or series of movements; 3. Habitual or vigorous activity; energy ("American Heritage", 1994, p. 8). The, the distinct difference between both ideas is that innovation fundamentally involves intense reflection, thought, and debate, whereas execution is nothing less than the application, facilitation, and implementation of all that has been thoroughly discussed.

Quantum Acad(yna^{E3})mics$^{SM®}$: Critical Thinking, The Vital Agent Which Fuses Innovation with Execution is an advanced critical thinking and predictive development certification workshop. It will eventually be utilized in a real-world context. It affords its residency-students (student body) several opportunities to research, assess, and investigate current theories and real world cases. It affords the opportunity, moreover, to reconstruct and reinvent the most prevalent current ways of thinking. It focuses thereon the growth and development of one's ability to engage in comprehensive CT; it is a concept called "Meta-cognition"—the comprehensive ongoing and cyclical critiquing of critical thinking. It endeavors to identify "explanations of individual differences in cognition" (Roberts & Ardos, 2010, "Abstract" section). Also, it is considered as "central to planning, problem-solving, evaluation and many aspects of language learning" (Kearsley, 2004-2010, "Introduction" section). In a nutshell, the workshop focuses thereon CT as the vital agent which fuses together the elements of innovation with execution. As a direct result, there will be the successful matriculation of a class of unparalleled thinkers whom are highly effective, highly skilled, and most competent agents of sociocultural, socioeconomic, and sociopolitical change.

Residency Background:

The—student body is comprised of American citizens deriving from a broad spectrum of cultural, ethnic, and religious backgrounds. This broad cultural-ethnicity spectrum includes: 1. Mexican, Hispanic, and Latin; 2. Biracial; 3. African-American; 4. European Indian; 5. Asian; 6. Native American; 7. Middle Eastern; 8. African; 9. Anglo-Saxon, and 10. European. Individually, they possess unique skill sets, abilities, and talents, inclusive of writing, singing, musicianship, athletics, and academics, journalism, research and development, and entrepreneurship, to name but a few. Concerning their academic-credentials, they have participated or are currently participating in junior college, undergraduate or graduate school studies.

The list of corresponding disciplines in which they possess specialized training includes: 1. Education; 2. Political Science; 3. Economics; 4. Finance and Accounting; 5.

History; 6. Psychology; 7. Counseling; 8. Fine 25 Arts; 9. Musical Theory. Regarding the personal attributes of the student body, they are both male and female, ranging from young adult-level to senior-level (average age, in fact, @ 35-42). They include individuals whom never have been exposed to the topic of CT, let alone meta-cognition. In short, they are best summarized as individuals who are adamant, eager, and passionate about understanding as well as further developing his or her own cerebral-cognitive abilities. Regarding the underlying motivation for participating in the comprehensive workshop, they desire to first and foremost increase and thus better themselves. It is a level of improvement which literally originates intrinsically, and then effectuates change upon the lives of all those who encounters them. Secondly to improve their ability that will lead to promotion within their current field of expertise.

Lastly, regarding the student body's prior exposure to CT as an essential bonding agent between innovation and execution, for a vast majority this is the first time. Thus, CT has existed for them as the meager ability to decide between one entity over and against the other. In other words, it is understood as an individual merely possessing the ability to engage therein decision-making, and thus arriving at a final conclusion relevant to which specific course, path, or choice to pursue. It addresses things which are otherwise positive, rather than the meager negativity. Professor Nosich (2005) reveals that CT consists of three fundamental parts: 1. Asking of questions; 2. Trying to answer 15 those questions by reasoning them out; 3. Believing the results of our reasoning (pp. 5-6).

Conversely, it does not include negativity, or emotionless activity, as it were. In fact, the very idea of CT existing without the presence of emotions is outright in error and expansively flawed. Professor Nosich further declares that the idea of "emotionless thinking" is at the least nothing more than a myth. He concedes that—Some emotions do indeed get in the way of critical thinking: rage and panic, for example. It is often extremely difficult for people to think clearly about a decision when they are enraged (Nosich, 2005, p. 15). In other words, by incorporating CT skills into a workshop through the utilization of computer software, internet capabilities, engaging in information gathering via research, active participation in safe, yet intensely challenging discourse sessions, and the interaction with a group mentor-instructor will inevitably result in students becoming highly effective, skilled, and competent comprehensive critical thinkers. In short, they will become individuals whom, here again, are well able to effectuate long-lasting positive change within the very contextual infrastructure, if you please, of their corresponding spheres of influence.

Ultimate Goal:

The ultimate goal of this workshop is the generation and matriculation of students whom are highly effective, highly skilled, and most competent critical thinkers (CT)—Masters of Hyper-meta Cognition[SM®].

They will possess not only a greater appreciation as well as understanding of innovation plus execution, as individual and interdependent elements of successful activity, rather they will be able to effectively apply this comprehensive knowledge into their corresponding spheres of influence—locally, regionally, nationally, and globally. In addition, they will have the necessary tools and resources for assisting other individuals in becoming comprehensive engagers-active participators of CT; these individuals will become passionate and philanthropic-mentors existing within their corresponding environments. In fact, if CT is lacking even the slightest in the "fusion interaction formula": innovation's affiliation and interaction with execution, success will more than likely never become realized. Nevertheless, CT exists as the fundamental impetus which postures the individual to not only identify the essential elements of innovation, but also discern the most feasible and correct time for actually implementing what has already been decided into the specific system for which it is intended. Professors Browne and Keeley (1998) admonishes that "Before we evaluate someone's reasoning, we must first find it" (p. 13). In short, if one has never endeavored to develop and train their CT muscles, he or she will be ill-equipped in identifying the pertinent core issues and thus arrive at a most desirable main objective.

Main Objectives:

In order to successfully matriculate throughout the breadth and length of this course, the residency-students are expected and required to:

1. Define critical thinking from their own individual perspective;
2. List their individual experiences in having to engage in some sort of decision-making;
3. Provide their own interpretation of what success is and what it mean to them at a personal-level;
4. Define wisdom from their own individual perspective;
5. List ways that they might interconnect wisdom, along with the overall concept of critical thinking;
6. Develop curriculum pertinent to their approach and understanding to critical thinking;
7. Read three peer-reviewed articles and write a summary paper providing their perspective of meta-cognition;
8. Participate in three critical debates within a group context.
9. Draft a final paper which describes how they intend on incorporating all that has been learned into their corresponding spheres of influence.

Workshop Curriculum:

Regarding the identification of a central task, as it were, it is best summarized by sub-dividing into two fundamental categories: 1. The vital parts or components of critical thinking; 2. The common and most prevalent impediments which often impedes upon critical thinking from becoming fully realized.

Pertinent to the first category, it—involves asking questions (Nosich, 2005, p. 5). The second category, moreover, comprise both "trying to answer those questions by reasoning them out" and "believing the results of our reasoning" (Nosich, 2005, p. pp. 5-6). In other words, the overarching principle involves the thought of critical thinking existing for, if no other purpose, than to equip its participators in addressing, exploring, inquiring, responding to, and solving the diverse challenges and issues considered pervading or prevalent. In short, the central task involves equipping its participating residents in becoming highly skilled, wholly balanced, and profoundly competent practitioners who effectuate lasting and constructive change in their corresponding spheres of influence.

Moreover, as it relates to the fundamental questions which are considered as most applicable to the aforementioned tasks, they are as follows: 1. What key content concepts and critical thinking skills or dispositions are needed to accomplish the task(s); 2. What types of instructional activities could help students acquire these skills and concepts; 3. How could critical thinking criteria be applied to assess student knowledge, skills, and 30 task performance, the answers are as follows.

Regarding question number one—key content concepts and skills or dispositions needed, in the order of importance: 1. All resident students have the potential for becoming highly successful critical thinkers; 2. What initially appears to be a challenge or deficiency actually is nothing less than a priceless asset for future utilization; 3. In order to become masters of critical thinking—meta-cognition, the individual must be willing to actively engage in the comprehensive training or purging process, as it were, from start to finish. Concerning the required abilities, dispositions, skills, and talents required, they include: a. Depth of character; b. Breadth of experience, inclusive of knowledge; c. Diligence and perseverance in remaining acute and precise throughout the entire process; d. Self-sufficiency that is the strength of character in persistently 10 remaining self-motivated; e. Self-discipline.

Nonetheless, all of the character attributes only further contributes to the overall success that will inevitably become realized, if the individual is willing to maximize every moment for critical conditioning, development, and training. Hence, the ultimate benefit of fully engaging every aforementioned attribute is for the sake of remaining firmly focused and totally committed upon the main or centralized point of view, pertinent to the corresponding discipline. Professor Nosich (2005) avers, in fact, the chief or underlying "point of view (or perspective) of a discipline runs so deep that it can seem as if practitioners of the discipline are seeing a different world from yours, and in a sense they are" (p. 114). The three essential things which results from seeing the 20 world from the right frame of reference are: 1. Seeing the items within the encompassing domain of the discipline; 2. Seeing them in terms of the concepts and categories of the discipline; 3. Seeing the connections among those items (Nosich, 2005, p. 114).

Regarding question number two—types of instructional activities, the recommend activities which students will participate includes ongoing question and answers sessions intended to afford participants the chance to challenge and critique one another, random surveys which provokes the students for outside of the box reflection and thinking, and lastly utilization of computerized training programs which begins with modestly inundating the student with a volume of pertinent information. Lastly, the final piece of activity involves the opportunity to engage in intense research and critical investigation pertinent to the relevant systematic parameters.

In other words, students will be afforded the opportunity to utilize diverse technology and computer systems in order retrieve critical and pertinent information which can be directly implementing, facilitated, and thus utilized within the context of the comprehensive training program itself. Lastly, regarding the third and final question—critical thinking criteria which can be applied for assessment purposes, it will, in a nutshell, involve the testing material divided into three rudimentary categories. These categories serves as the *nuts and bolts* on both the design and facilitation of the testing assessment, relevant to the student's past and current levels of knowledge, skills, and task performance.

Moreover, the first category is titled or labeled as the "Instruction" Phase. In short, this phase involves the assessment and overall tabulation of the student's depth and breadth of relevant academic knowledge. It tests and assesses the overall quality of information which has been processed and stored for future utilization by the student, applicable to his or her career or field of specialization. The second category is known or referred to as the "Application" Phase. It involves the actual application of the information that has been received, hence processed for future application, facilitation, and utilization. The final category is known as the "Hyper-meta Cognition" Phase. In short, it involves the ongoing quest of seeking alternative, novel, and innovative ways for improving the encompassing critical thinking-reflection process, from start to finish.

TOPIC 1—Fundamental Components-Parts of CT:

Topic 1 Objectives

At the concluding phase of this workshop, the student will be able to:

1. Recite and articulate the essential components of CT.
2. Create a list of core questions considered both relevant and vital to CT
3. Application to individual sphere of influence.

Topic 1 Introduction

What exactly is this notion of critical thinking? Does it involve nothing more than the creation of questions considered important and relevant to the challenges or issues at-hand? Or, is it nothing more than the process of engaging into a system of checks and balances, that is the essential activity of separating things considered important from things considered insignificant. The truth is, the critical thinking, at its most rudimentary level includes all of the aforementioned. In fact, Professor Nosich avers that critical thinking is a quasi-dimensional activity; it "is thinking about your thinking, while your thinking, in order to make your thinking better" (Nosich, 2005, p. 2). It is comprised of the following CT-related features: 1. It is reflective; 2. It involves standard; 3. It is authentic; 4. It involves being reasonable. It involves the ongoing activity of drafting what is considered as relevant questions. A list of questions that is required in order to effectively address and respond to the diverse challenges-issues that initiated the process from the start.

A brief list of the most feasible or right questions are:

1. What are the issues and the conclusions?
2. What are the reasons?
3. What words or phrases are ambiguous?

4.   Are there any fallacies in the reasoning?

5.   What reasonable conclusions are possible? (Browne & Keeley, 1998, p. 15 12)

As it relates to the three main components of CT, for starters, "critical thinking involves asking questions, it—involves trying to answer those questions by reasoning them out", and it also—involves believing the results of our reasoning (Browne & Keeley, 2005, pp. 5-6). In short, critical thinking is the process in which one engages for the purpose of developing his or her ability to navigate through diverse challenges and issues, and ultimately arrive at what is considered as the most acceptable solution plan.

TOPIC 2—Impediments to Critical Thinking:

Topic 2 Objectives

At the concluding phase of this workshop, the student will be able to:

1.   Recite and articulate the main impediments to CT.

2.   Create a list of core questions considered both relevant and vital to CT

3.   Application to individual sphere of influence.

Topic 2 Introduction

Impediments to CT can be classified as anything which blocks, hinders, impedes, obstructs, or retards comprehensive critical thinking from materializing. In other words, it can exist as any challenge, issue, or person which will ultimately get in the way of full and complete critical thought development from occurring. In short, it can be the very factor which makes the difference between success and failure. And in a worst case scenario, it can even make the key factor that in a financial or monetary language, will literally add up to tens of thousands or even a hundred thousand dollars. Hence, a prime example of one of the deeper and more pervasive impediments is egocentrism. It is understood as self-centered type of thinking which literally "interferes with critical thinking on all levels, from the deepest to the most superficial" (Nosich, 10 2005, p. 24).

A brief list of the more common or prevalent impediments to CT includes: 1. Forming a picture of the world on the basis of the news; 2. Forming a picture of the world on the basis of movies, TV, advertising, magazines; 3. All or nothing thinking; 4. Us-versus-them thinking; 5. Stereotyping; 6. Fears (Nosich, 2005, pp. 21-23). In short, an impediment to critical thinking is anything obstacles or negative expression—inclusive of mindsets, which hinders high performing CT from becoming fully realized.

TOPIC 3—Asking the Right Questions:

Topic 3 Objectives

At the concluding phase of this workshop, the student will be able to:

1. Engage in a series of critical thinking discourses which ultimately results in the right questions being asked and addressed.
2. Articulate the essential necessity of drafting the right questions
3. Draft a list of core questions which are considered applicable to the diverse challenges and issues pervading one's current field of expertise.

Topic Introduction

The main reason that justifies the need for engaging into a series of critical or vital question identification is for the sake of addressing, confronting, and thus dealing with all possible challenges or issues which might impede upon comprehensive critical thinking from becoming realized. After all, the contemporary times in which we live and function are fast becoming inundated with such a plethora of problems that immediate resolution is a rare commodity. It is a quandary that requires effective critical thinkers wising up and affording plus providing solutions to the main challenges and issues both pervading and permeating our society. It is the essential cure for the corresponding systemic pandemic of the critical thinking class, or lack thereof. In other words, the fundamental activity of engaging in asking the process of asking the right critical questions, it essentially "consists of an awareness of a set of interrelated critical questions, plus the ability and willingness to ask and answer them at appropriate times" (Browne & Keeley, 1998, p. 2). In short, having the ability to effectively address and thus respond to the right questions, can literally mean the difference between comprehensive and lasting victory, or conversely falling into the pit of perpetual and never-ending frustration.

TOPIC 4—Current Theories of Thinking and Learning:

Topic Objectives

At the concluding phase of this workshop, the student will be able to:

1. List at three major theories which directly correlate to the field of thinking and learning.
2. Engage in open discussion concerning the fundamental particulars of each theoretical framework.
3. Identify the weakness of deficiencies within each theoretical model.
4. Identify the strengths evident within each theoretical model.
5. Discuss the intricacies of the 'Power-Load-Margin' formula.

Topic Introduction:

Critical thinking is so important in addressing and thus responding to the quandary of challenges and issues which often plaques the very core of our society. In fact, it is the ability for individuals to effectively address, navigate, and thus sort through and filter through the conundrum of problems which otherwise hinder and thus impose upon corresponding solutions from becoming wholly realized. Peter A. Facione, (2010) 30 professes that CT involves the "Teaching people to make good decisions and you equip them to improve their own futures and become contributing members of society, rather than burdens on society" (p. 3). In short, effective critical thinking is nothing less than the ability of an individual or group of individuals rightly applying sound and balanced discretion as well as judicial understanding.

Pertinent to the discussion of critical thinking frameworks, it is best summarized as the avenues or systems of thought in which individuals often endeavor in order to sort through and thus arrive at a most acceptable plus feasible working solution. A list of pertinent critical thinking models includes: 1. Transformational Theory of Thinking and Learning; 2. Theory of Margin; 3. Andragogy Model of Adult Thinking and Learning.

To begin with, the theory of transformative learning—developed in 1978 by Jack 10 Mezirow, fundamentally approaches thinking and learning as an ongoing and perpetual process of growth, development, and transformation—physically, psychologically, and emotionally. In short, it professes that "transformative learning occurs when individuals change their frames of reference by critically reflecting on their assumptions and beliefs and consciously making and implementing plans that bring about new ways of defining their worlds" (Imel, 1998, ¶8, p. 2). It involves the holistic metamorphosis which often occurs within an individually at the deepest and most intrinsic-level.

The second theory of thinking and learning is called the—Theory of Margin. It was developed and first proposed Professor Howard McClusky in 1924. It essentially centers around the notion that "being an adult means facing continuous growth, change, and integration, in which constant effort must be made to use the energy available for meeting normal living responsibilities" (2002, ¶1, p. 1). In other words, the corresponding critical "factors of adult life are the load the adult carries in living, and the power that is available to him or her to carry" (2002, ¶3, p. 1). In short, it is a quite simple—power margin formula that establishes a working correlation between the load and the availability of power to carry the load; it exists as $M = L/P$. Hence, it is defined as the—greater the power in relationship to the load the more margin of power will essentially be made available for tapping therein. The third and final theory, as developed and pioneered by Malcolm Knowles, is thus entitled as—The Theory of Andragogy. It involves, at the most elemental core, "the understanding of how adults learn" (Lieb, 1991, ¶1, p. 1), as well as engage in activity which requires critical thinking as well as critical reflection.

In other words, it delves into the core infrastructure which essentially supports the comprehensive system of thinking in which that same individual consistently and actively engages therein. In short, it consists of the following systematic attributes which collectively comprises the basic and elemental components of the comprehensive system: 1. Adults are autonomous and self-directed; 2. Adults possess priceless and diverse life experiences and knowledge; 3. Adults are goal-oriented; 4. Adults are relevancy-oriented; 5. Adults are practical. Thus, it is an independent, yet wholly interdependent and highly functional system in which all relevant components must function or else the system itself will become both dysfunctional and handicapped.

Learning Environment

Home—the place where, when you go there, they have to take you in (McLellan quoting Frost, 1998, p. 87).

First of all, before endeavoring to teach, and thus afford learners as well as students the necessary tools and resources required for effective critical thinking, it is of extreme importance to create a vital learning environment. It is a place where participating individuals—facilitators of learning as well as residency-students, are afforded great flexibility and leeway in challenging others in critical debate and discourse. It also includes the provision of expansive room for comprehensive, personal growth, development, and maturation—emotionally, physically, and psychologically. Again, it is a process that is both *multi-tiered and quasi-dimensional* in context and character.

Secondly, regarding the necessity for allowing open critical debate for the sake of development and training in the courseroom environment,—it must be conducive to the encouragement of critical thinking and the development of critical thinking skills (Leicester, 2010, p. 102). In other words, it ought to both encourage and challenge students to become ideal critical thinkers whom are disposed to try to get it right,' to present a position honestly and clearly, and to care about the worth and dignity of every person; furthermore the ideal critical thinker has the ability to clarify, to seek and judge well the basis for a view, to infer wisely from the basis, to imaginatively suppose and integrate, and to do these things with a deep sense and resolve for dispatch, sensitivity, and rhetorical skill (Ennis, 2000, p. 2, summary and contents).

Next, in the process of engaging therein a context of a safe and highly challenging learning environment, it ought to be expected that good and strong relationships will be erected between—teacher and pupils, and pupil and pupil (Leicester, 2010, p. 102). In other words, if respect does not first exist within and thus originate from the teacher, hence facilitator of learning, then any expectation of similar character attributes, reflective of both upright character and integrity is outright ridiculous and at the very least despicable. Moreover, the end result of participating in such an environment is the generation and matriculation, the rising up of a next generation of critical thinkers whom are highly effective facilitators of comprehensive positive change and development within their corresponding spheres of influence.

Lastly, it is a current theory of action better known as "Cerebral-Citizens, the by-product of Quantum Acad(yna^{E3})mics$^{SM®}$". Moreover, a theory of action is defined by Argyris and Schön (1974) as—a theory of deliberate human behavior, which is for the agent a theory of control but which, when attributed to the agent, also serves to explain or predict his behavior (p. 6). It is, in short, a comprehensive and quasi-dimensional process which serves if for no other purpose than the matriculation of successful leaders whom are progenitors of comprehensive change within their corresponding spheres of influence—socio-culturally, socio-economically, socio-politically, and socio-spiritually.

Instructional Strategies

The first place to start, as it relates to the development of instructional strategies, is the open and candid discussion intended to identify diverse plus alternative strategies of learning. These newly developed strategies, over the course of time, will become 25 implemented and thus inserted into the overall workshop system-curriculum. In other words, the main objective involves two central activities, the—identifying and challenging assumptions, and exploring alternative ways of thinking and acting (Brookfield, 1987, p. 71). In short, it attempts to create and thus facilitate a comprehensive working system which endeavors to afford both teacher and students the necessary tools and resources 30 essential for solving diverse issues and problems. As a direct result, the workshop will 39 both produce and generate a class of "cerebral citizens" whom are most effective in solving seemingly impossible challenges, difficulties, and problems which otherwise would be left ignored, isolated, and unresolved.

A list of highly recommended strategies includes:

- **High impact Motivational Sessions**: This initial activity includes both open debate and critical discourse. It begins with group members briefly introducing themselves, followed by open floor "round table" critical debate and discourse. Each member is afforded an equal opportunity for addressing and vocalizing areas of concern, inclusive of issues, as well as the opportunity to challenge one another. This occurs, in short, for the sake of providing diversity of perspectives and ways of thinking, all of which is essential in arriving at the most acceptable or feasible solution pertinent to the main challenge, issue, or problem. In the end, it attempts to uncover, and respond to "the assumptions underlying our most comfortable ways of thinking and acting" which is otherwise a "difficult and frequently unnerving activities" (Brookfield, 1987, p. 90); it delves into and thus attempts to reconstruct and perhaps even reinvent our undergirding structures of learning. Brookfield (1987) affirms that the overall process of "Teaching critical thinking is thus inherently disruptive and involves intentionally creating an atmosphere of disequilibrium, so that students can change, rework, or reconstruct their thinking process'" (p. 90).

- **Role Play and Simulations**: This second activity attempts to afford learners the opportunity to participate in real world case scenarios. It involves group members alternating between diverse character roles, all with the underlying attempt for affording the priceless opportunity for acquiring and thus developing essential critical thinking character traits-attributes. It is an arduous and otherwise challenging activity that exists as nothing less than a balancing act involving both critical thinking protagonists and critical thinking antagonists.

    In short,—this balancing act can be rehearsed through role plays and simulations, but it can be effectively developed only through actual practice (Brookfield, 1987, p. 73). In order for it to be a successful endeavor, it will "require helpers to examine their 30 own activities critically and to be ready to learn from their mistakes" (Brookfield, 1987, p. 73); it require two fundamental success traits: 1. Unwavering commitment; 2. All consuming passionate desire to follow through all the way, until the desired result is wholly achieved and realized.

- **Reflective Analysis**: This third activity is best described as the opportunity for individual participants to get together on a one-to-one basis. While conversing and engaging in much needed critical dialogue, each participant is afforded a window of time to fully and unapologetically express one's own random ideas, insights, opinions, and perspectives. This activity actually continues for a previously agreed upon time frame, yet it alternates between each individual, whom engages as communicator and sounding board. In regards to the personality of the environment, it is mutually respectful, yet of modestly high-impact regarding either the affirmation of one's personal perspective or conversely the outright rejection and unbiased critiquing thereof. It also consists of relevant divergent recommendations, essentially intended to afford all active participants the priceless opportunity for critically analyzing the alternative perspectives of their counterparts.

- **Open and Unfiltered Personal Expression**: This fourth and final activity is considered by Professor Brookfield (1987) declares that "One of the most useful tasks we can perform as we seek to develop critical thinking in other people is to reflect back to them their attitudes, rationalizations, and habitual ways of thinking and acting" (p. 75). In other words, each individual student is provided the opportunity to candidly and openly express his or her own unique critical thinking-inspired point of view. That is, each student is encouraged to openly discuss and articulate his or her relevant critical thinking ideas, insights, opinions, and perspectives to their collective student body of peers and colleagues. The main purpose for this, number one, is to establish such a modestly intimidating and pressing environment-setting where their innate apprehensions, fears, and uncertainties can be addressed, challenged, and eventually overcome and thus fully resolved.

The second main purpose for engaging in this activity is to allow one's peer and colleagues to pinpoint, address and offer diverse strategies for considering and perhaps even implementing alternative ways of learning and thinking. It serves to afford each participant a mirror of sorts, in order to "see oneself in new ways, from a range of different vantage points" (Brookfield, 1987, p. 75). Thus it inevitably attempts to "distill what we are learning from the challenges and supports of our world" (Ibid). Regarding, in summary, it affords each critical thinker a way of escape from being otherwise trapped in his or her otherwise overlooked and taken-for-granted archive-database of assumptions. We are, in essence, able to rightly distinguish between what is real and what is an illusion, what it truth and what is error, and finally what is contaminated and what is pure, unbiased, and objective logical reasoning.

Learning Assessment Instruments:

The preferred selection of diverse assessment instruments fall under three chief categories: 1. Good Practice Audit (GPA); 2. Critical Incident Questionnaires (CIQ); 3. Appreciative Inquiry Worksheet (AIW).

Regarding the first instrument—GPA, for starters it serves to afford a process which attempts to create a collaborative setting in which problems are addressed, discussed, and ultimately resolved. It is "a three phase process in which teachers search their experiences for good resources to common problems they encounter" (Brookfield, 1995, p. 161). In other words, as it relates to both the underlying structure of the discussion process, it involves an amalgamation of "individual reflection and collaborative critical analysis and is focused on helping people deal with difficulties they have themselves identified" (Ibid). While endeavoring to engage in much needed critical dialogue and critical reflection, the relevant participants experience critical reflection, open and candid sharing, and comprehensive reflective analysis. In short, the overall and encompassing process consists of three elemental phases: 1. Problem formulation; 2. Individual and collective analysis; 3. Compilation of suggestions for practice. Also, it must be mentioned that even though the audit was initially designed for educators, it can be slightly adjusted or modified so that it directly applies to the corresponding particulars relevant to the residency students.

Regarding the second instrument—CIQ fundamentally helps us to embed our teaching in accurate information about students'learning that is regularly solicited and anonymously given (Brookfield, 1995, p. 114). Pertinent to the structural layout of the questionnaire, it exists as "a single page form that is handed out to students at the end of the last class", it includes five simple and straight forward questions—each of which asks students to write down some details about events that happened in the class during that corresponding week of activity (Brookfield, 1995, p. 114).

A brief list of relevant questions which often comprise the CIQ includes:

1. At what moment did you feel most engaged within the context of what was taking place within the courseroom?
2. At what moment did you feel most distanced from what was taking place within the courseroom?
3. What action that anyone took in the class this week did you find most alarming and helpful?
4. What action that anyone took in the class this week did you find most puzzling or confusing?
5. What specific key points do you find most applicable to your current working sphere of influence?
6. What specific recommendation would you make and thus submit for the sake of improving the overall quality of the workshop learning experience?
7. In comparison to the person you were on day one of the workshop, what fundamental changes have occurred within the context of your own life?

In short, the most important benefit of student participating in the CIQ is so that the fundamental dynamics of the workshop can be addressed, confronted, and ultimately, if considered of urgent necessity, revised, reinvented, or reconstructed all for the sake of becoming a more effective learning experience.

Regarding the final instrument—AIW, it fundamentally exists with the chief purpose of engaging in—an ongoing process for investigating and understanding critical organization issues . . . it provokes and stimulates: 1. Organization members' interest and ability in exploring critical issues using evaluation logic; 2. Organization members' involvement in evaluative processes, and; 3. The personal and professional growth of individuals within the organization (Preskill & Catsambas, 2006, p. 39).

Moreover, it focuses thereon the evaluators being equipped in assessing and documenting students involvement and performance; specifically it addresses and "responds to the evolving requirements of those who duct evaluations" (Ibid, p. 41). In other words, it wholly ensures that applicable evaluators are provided—a direction for the evaluation that was more constructive than it might have been had another process been used (Ibid, p. 73). Regarding the main goals of the AIW, it addresses and concentrates thereon two fundamental components of the comprehensive evaluative process: 1. The 4-D Model; 2. The 4-I Model. As discussed in one of the previous paragraphs, the 4-D Model includes the following four phases; 1. Discovery; 2. Dreaming; 3 Designing; 4. Destiny. Whereas, the 4-I Model includes the following four phases: 1. Inquire; 2. Imagine; 3. Innovate; 4. Implement (Preskill, 2006, p. 8, slide 10). In the end, the main benefit of utilizing the Appreciative Inquiry Worksheet is to essentially—add to existing evaluation systems, or develop new evaluation systems (Ibid, p. 15, slide 30).

Conclusion:

AI; it is defined as—a group process that inquiries into, identifies, and further develops the best of what is' in organizations in order to create a better future (Preskill 20 & Catsambas, 2006, p. 1). It affords the relevant decision making parties the requisite particulars for ensuring that the required energy, resources, and time invested produces, in the end, quantified-dividends. Pertinent to the chief objective of this course project, it fundamentally requires that two fundamental components exist, both of which are necessary for comprehensive success to become realized, it includes: 1. Innovation, and; 2. Execution.

Quantum Acad(yna^E3)mics^SM®: Critical Thinking, The "Vital Agent Which Fuses Innovation with Execution" is a critical thinking plus predictive development workshop. It affords its residency-students (student body) several opportunities to research, assess, and investigate current theories and real world cases. The ultimate goal of this workshop is the generation and matriculation of students whom are highly effective, highly skilled, and most competent critical thinkers (CT)—Masters of Hyper-meta Cognition^SM®. They will possess not only a greater appreciation and well as understanding of innovation plus execution, as individual and sometimes interdependent elements of successful activity, rather they will be able to effectively apply this comprehensive knowledge into their corresponding spheres of influence—locally, regionally, nationally, and globally. In order for the students to successfully matriculate throughout the breadth and length of this course, they are expected and required to complete and thus fulfill nine main objectives.

Regarding the identification of a central task, as it were, it is best summarized by sub-diving into two fundamental categories: 1. The vital parts or components of critical thinking; 2. The common and most prevalent impediments which often impedes upon critical thinking from becoming fully realized. All of the character attributes, nonetheless, only further contributes to the overall success that will inevitably become realized, if the individual is willing to maximize every moment for critical conditioning, development, and training. Anyhow, pertinent to the learning environment, before endeavoring to teach, and thus afford learners as well as students the necessary tools and resources required for effective critical thinking, it is of extreme importance to create a vital learning environment.

Next, pertinent to the instructional strategies, the first place to start, as it relates to the development of instructional strategies, is the open and candid discussion intended to identify diverse plus alternative strategies of learning. These newly developed strategies, over the course of time, will become implemented and thus inserted into the overall workshop system-curriculum. Lastly, pertinent to the Learning Assessment Instruments, the preferred selection of diverse assessment instruments fall under three chief categories:

1. Good Practice Audit (GPA); 2. Critical Incident Questionnaires ((CIQ); Appreciative Inquiry Worksheet (AIW).

Quantum Acad(ynaE3)micsSM®: Critical Thinking, The Vital Agent Which Fuses Innovation with Execution, in a nutshell, focuses thereon critical thinking as the vital agent which fuses together innovation with execution. Hence, the chief objective of the comprehensive workshop is the successful matriculation of a class of unparalleled thinkers whom are highly effective, highly skilled, and most competent agents of sociocultural, socioeconomic, and sociopolitical change.

Summary of Critiquing Peer/Colleagues Course Project:

Perhaps the most effective strategy for addressing the final aspect of this comprehensive course project assignment is with summarizing his critiquing of a colleague/peer through the following statement "focusing thereon the positive components above and beyond all else". That is, the underlying theme or main objective involves the concentration upon that in which the author—Linda Spier, mentioned and thus embedded within the context of her final course project.

In short, Professor Claude E. Bonet submitted comments to the author which directly addresses that in which he considered as the most important or fundamental strengths of the overall written draft submission; it is best identified as Mr. Bonet's working theory in action rightly entitled as "The 10 Comprehensive Yet Concise Critiquing of a Project from a Holistic Frame of Reference". In short, it focuses primarily upon which ought to be considered as the foundational, plus philosophical infrastructure upon which the academic work is essentially considered erected thereon. Anyhow, a "theory of action" is defined as a theory of deliberate human behavior, which is for the agent a theory of control but which, when attributed to the agent, also serves to "explain or predict his behavior" (Argyris & Schön, 1974, p. 6).

Pertinent to the distinct classes or categories in which the comprehensive critique is listed they are accordingly:

1. The overall impression upon which the project made upon the reader;
2. Critique of the author's creation of the overall structure and presentation 20 of the project;
3. The logic identified within the context of the course project;
4. Author's ability and effectiveness at constructing the course project from a master craftsmen or mason's point-of-view;
5. Direct relevance identified or constructed between author's vantage point and the main theme of the course project.

Regarding the first class—the overall impression made by the author (Linda Spier), it is safe to declare the she was most effective in creating and thus generating on overall lasting impression. In other words, the author was most effective in establishing a revitalizing experience, one that includes critical component applicable to critical thinking in an adult learning context. For example, the author stated "It is essential that any learner enrolled in an Introductory Psychology course develop the ability to use critical thinking, which entails the use of higher-order thinking skills to evaluate complex research problems" (Spier, L. August 29, 2010). This statement was then reinforced with a citing by Brookfield. It reads that, "According to Brookfield (1987, p. 23) as a process, critical thinking is not purely passive . . . it involves alternating phases of analysis and action" (Ibid). In short, the work was both thought-provoking and at the very least richly informative.

Regarding the second class—author's creation of the overall structure and presentation of the project, the author (Linda Spier) did a marvelous job of covering or presenting what is considered as pertinent and vital aspects relevant to the core theme of critical thinking incorporated into the discipline or course called Psychology-Counseling.

In other words, the author was successful in drafting and identifying the underlying link between the course itself and the overall discussion of critical thinking in an adult learning context. For example, the author stated the "objectives identified in the workshop lay the foundation for demonstrating" (Spier, Aug. 29, 2010).

In my opinion, this statement was indeed most poignant and foundational. That is, in regards to the idea of something being considered foundational, it appears that you did approach the overall project with the mindset and skills of a master craftsman—perhaps you are familiar with the overall approach of such a profession. In short, Linda Spier did a good job in affording the essential correlation between the course workshop and the academic discipline for which it is intended to effectuate constructive change therein.

Regarding the third class—the logic identified, the author appeared to have begun the most elemental-level, in mentioning the essential background particulars of the project. It is, in short, clear, concise, succinct, yet filled with volumes of key information.

Regarding the fourth class—the course project being constructed from a master craftsmen or mason's point-of-view, the author appears to have utilized a "level-upon-level" approach; it is structurally laid out with the a logical that flows from one paragraph unto the next. For example, in the paragraph entitled "Curriculum" Linda Spier addressed the fundamentals concerning "this workshop concentrates on asking the question, "How can we most effectively teach the learners to use critical thinking in order to—think like a psychologist" (Spier, L., August 29, 2010). Thus, what was addressed briefly in this, was dealt with in much further and substantive detail in the paragraph thus entitled "Learning Environment", as she cited Brookfield; it is listed that "When an instructor considers their teaching style and philosophy they must understand the impact of what Brookfield (1995) calls the four lenses,—(1) our autobiographies as teachers and learners, (2) our students' eyes, (3) our colleagues' experiences, and (4) theoretical literature (p 29)".

Regarding the final class—direct relevance identified or constructed, applicable to the four aforementioned bullets, it literally correlates to the nuts and bolts of psychology. In other words, is psychology or the overall discussion thereof about nothing less than the color of lens in which the active participators engages, facilitates and hence utilizes. In short, I am most intrigued by the way the author threaded the paragraphs together in such a way that it is easy to alternate between the lens of the student (current) and the evolving psychologist (future).

Working Topic and Thesis Statement:

The underlying and overarching theme is a major crisis occurring within the comprehensive educational system's current context. The crisis has become so critically dire that the need for immediate and massive change is considered a pragmatically urgent necessity requiring immediate and an unwavering response. The main notion or topic is that lasting and ongoing success is a progressively evolving process. Hence, the main objective includes verifying and identifying a distinct research topic, as well as delving into, and addressing the three main themes wholly reinforced by sound factual; there is a major crisis occurring within the current educational system.

In short, the chief route through which lasting change best occurs is with developing a plan that addresses all issues pertinent to the vastly diverse challenges and issues prevalent within the collective educational system. Thus, ongoing and lasting success is possible; however, it requires the investment of sufficient levels of energy, time, and other critical resources, all of which are fundamentally discussed within the context of the three core article-assignment themes.

Identification of the Three Core Themes:

The three core themes are identified as common threads existing between the three pre-selected articles include: 1. The educational system—past and current context—is in dire need of major systematic overhaul plus comprehensive reform; 2. The method utilized pays a critical and major role in the overall efficacy of reformation; 3. Motivation of all corresponding parties—administrators and student body—is imperative.

The *first theme* asserts that in order for lasting change to occur, active commitment and diligent participation by all corresponding parties is required. Thus, a major crisis has irrefutably been ongoing for such an overextended period of time—within the field of academics at all levels—that the only way for any positive change and success to become truly realized, immediate engagement must occur right now.

The *second theme* reveals that the method or methods utilized plays a critical and major role in the overall reformation efficacy, it is important to carefully invest the necessary energy and time. Thus, the main purpose is to assess the gathered results pertinent to effectuating comprehensive school reform, applicable to overall student achievement. In short, there is indeed a direct correlation-connection between the selected method utilized—by the team of corresponding academic investigative researchers—as well as the overall quality of the results thereof.

The *final theme* assures that student involvement and active contribution towards lasting success should never be overlooked or even devalued. In short, student engagement is considered so critical and vital that Gross reveals that is a major priority in the overall consideration, formulation, and tabulation process.

Dire Need for Overhaul & Reformation:

Gross et al. (2009) avers, and asserts that "the appeal of schoolwide reform (which was widely touted as a response to the poor outcomes of earlier reforms that came across as fragmented and disjointed) was evident in the rapid expansion of the movement in its earliest years" (p. 111). That is, the first place in which active participation must occur is at the administrative-level. Hence, it is an idea referred to as the underlying efficacy of school administrator's self-efficacy. In other words, any endeavor to facilitate 30 major academic reform first requires that the team of pertinent school administrator's be able to effectively facilitate—self-referent judgments of his/her—capabilities to organize and execute courses of action required' (p. 396) for successful school leadership and reaching desired school outcomes (McCollum et al. citing Bandura, 1986; 2009, p. 30).

Moreover, comprehensive school reformation is indeed a possible reality if it is irrefutably understood that there is an urgent, not to mention pressing crisis within the current academic-educational systems. It requires immediate and unwavering attention. It also requires that pertinent critical individuals respond in such a way characterized by innovation, as well as ongoing creative and flexible proactive responsiveness. In other words, "because of these [unique and ever fluctuating] dynamics, and the increasing frequency and speed of associate d transitions, coaching has evolved as a methodology to fill a need for growth as well as continuity in our lives" (Hart et al., 2001, p. 229). In short, the critical and urgent need for major and comprehensive plus systematic overhaul and reform will result in ongoing and lasting success if immediate action is actively engaged without further delay, haste, or trepidation. Hence, immediate attention is required in order for any positive maturation—change, development, growth to become fully realized.

Underlying Methods Considered Both Pragmatic & Vital:

Gross et al. (2009) also reveals—pertinent to the notion of underlying methods that "our analysis of federal funding for CSR examines the grants' effects on reading and math achievement in a variety of student-level analyses" (p. 115). As a direct result of utilizing the selected research method—231 Texas elementary schools (about 6% of the total number of Texas primary schools as reported in the 2001-2002 school year) received grants to implement CSR designs, with statewide awards totaling more than $60 million (p. 115). Thus, McCollum and Kajs clearly appear to reinforce this alleged notion with sharing the results of their study; the results fundamentally assert that a distinct pattern indeed occurs. In fact, all of the dimensions of efficacy are statistically significantly positively correlated with mastery goal orientations (p. 37). Therefore, it is wholly and concretely upon that comprehensive and lasting success requires, if nothing else, that the "combinations of predictors—such as performance-approach orientation, mastery-approach orientation, and mastery-avoidance orientation (as a negative predictor) serve to indicate the highest levels of efficaciousness for some of the dimensions of efficacy in the SAES", also commonly referred to as the School Administrator Efficacy Scale.

This same SAES, in fact—germane to the 1988 Hawkins-Stafford Elementary and Secondary School Improvement Amendments to Chapter—allowed for schoolwide programs with Chapter 1 funds, the number of schoolwide programs more than tripled in the 1st year (Gross et al., 2009, p. 111).

The underlying notion is that there irrefutably exist a direct correlation-connection between overall success, and the array of selected method(s) both considered and facilitated. Hence, the overall quality of the gathered and collected results can be grossly affected by the quality of the method being considered and actively utilized. In short, it is critical and vital to invest the necessary energy and time to thoroughly assess the results and it relates to the main set of objectives which initiated and thus predicated reformation for the onset.

Importance of Key Players Possessing Unwavering Motivation:

Professor Gross and company concedes that—our analysis takes advantage of student-level panel data that not only allow us to test the effect of the awards over an extended period of time but also offer a couple of key advantages only available with student-level data (Gross et al., 2009, p. 113).

This very same notion or concept, moreover, of required motivation of all participating parties—administrators and student body "it is nothing less than—a complex, multidimensional construct that can vary widely, and is difficult to pinpoint" (McCollum, 2009, p. 29). In fact, in regards to the specific motivational theories considered feasible and applicable; the list includes "self-efficacy theory (e.g. Bandura, 1986) achievement goal orientation theory (e.g. Elliot & McGregor, 2001) and attribution theory (Weiner, 1986)" (McCollum and Kajs, 2009, p. 29). Conversely, for the sake of establishing a critical, as well as wholly pragmatic link between the joint idea of: 1. Motivation; 2. Utilization of coaching as an alternative modality within the context of innovative educational reform. Next, Hart et al. (2001) divulge that "the coach's orientation is prospective, focusing on goals, untapped potential, and critical success factors in a whole person who seeks to maximize his or her fulfillment in life and work" (p. 230). In short, lasting and permanent or irreversible success, within the context of the academic and educational system is not only an ongoing and progressively evolving process requiring all key players or participators to not only identify the main goal or objective, but more importantly mandates both a quality of untiring and unwavering commitment to follow through all the way to the final phase, the finish line of official completion.

Conclusion:

The crisis has become so critically dire that the need for immediate and massive change is considered a pragmatically urgent necessity requiring immediate and an unwavering response. Ongoing and lasting success is possible; yet, most importantly it requires the investment of sufficient levels of energy, time, and other critical resources, all of which are fundamentally discussed within the context of the three core article-assignment themes.

The first theme asserts that in order for lasting change to occur, active commitment and diligent participation by all corresponding parties is required. The second theme reveals that the method or methods utilized plays a critical and major role in the overall reformation efficacy—it is important to carefully invest the necessary energy and time. The final theme assures that student involvement and active contribution towards lasting success should never be overlooked or even devalued.

Regarding the dire need for overhaul and reformation, the first place in which active participation must occur is at the administrative-level; immediate attention is required in order for any positive maturation—change, development, growth to become fully realized. Regarding the underlying methods considered pragmatic and vital, the underlying notion is that there irrefutably exist a direct correlation-connection between overall success, and the array of selected method(s) considered and thus facilitated. Regarding the importance of key players possessing unwavering motivation, lasting and permanent or irreversible success is an ongoing and progressively evolving process. It requires all key players-participators to identify the main goal-objective, as well as mandating such a quality of untiring and unwavering commitment to follow through all the way to the final phase.

[Annotative Literature Overview]

Main Idea and Underlying Themes:

The overarching idea or main notion is that ongoing and progressively evolving success at all levels of the academic-educational system is possible. However, it requires the diligent and unwavering investment of substantive energy, time, and diverse other pertinent resources. There are three main themes which appear and exist within the context of all related articles. The first theme involves the vital urgency or dire need for major overhaul and systematic reformation, in a most expeditious manner. The second identifiable theme involves the identification, as well as active plus unwavering utilization of effective methods, essentially considered both critical and vital necessity of all corresponding players possessing an evidence of both breadth and depth of authentic motivation; it is considered vitally important.

Theme one—dire need for overhaul and reformation.
Requires active commitment and diligent participation.
Gross, B., Booker, T.K., & Goldhaber, D. (2009). Boosting student achievement: The effect of comprehensive school reform on student achievement. Educational Evaluation and Policy Analysis, 31(2), 111-126.
Any endeavor to facilitate reform school administrator's requisites.
Gross, B., Booker, T.K., & Goldhaber, D. (2009). Boosting student achievement: The effect of comprehensive school reform on student achievement. Educational Evaluation and Policy Analysis, 31(2), 111-126.
McCollum, D.L., Kais, L.T. (2009). Examining the relationship between school administrators' efficacy and goal orientations. Educational Research Quarterly, 32(3), 29-46.

Theme two—methods utilized considered critical and major.
Importance of investing necessary energy and time. Gross, B., Booker, T.K., & Goldhaber, D. (2009). Boosting student achievement: The effect of comprehensive school reform on student achievement. Educational Evaluation and Policy Analysis, 31(2), 111-126.

McCollum, D.L., Kais, L.T. (2009). Examining the relationship between school administrators' efficacy and goal orientations. Educational Research Quarterly, 32(3), 29-46.

Vital requirement of combination of predictors. Gross, B., Booker, T.K., & Goldhaber, D. (2009). Boosting student achievement: The effect of comprehensive school reform on student achievement. Educational Evaluation and Policy Analysis, 31(2), 111-126.

Theme three—motivation of all parties considered imperative.

Student contribution and involvement ought to be given attention and concentration.

Gross, B., Booker, T.K., & Goldhaber, D. (2009). Boosting student achievement: The effect of comprehensive school reform on student achievement. Educational Evaluation and Policy Analysis, 31(2), 111-126.

McCollum, D.L., Kais, L.T. (2009). Examining the relationship between school administrators' efficacy and goal orientations. Educational Research Quarterly, 32(3), 29-46.

Motivation theories considered feasible and applicable.

McCollum, D.L., Kais, L.T. (2009). Examining the relationship between school administrators' efficacy and goal orientations. Educational Research Quarterly, 32(3), 29-46.

Provision of a critical and pragmatic link.

Hart, V., Blattner, J., & Leipsic, S. (2001). Coaching versus therapy: A perspective. Consulting Psychology Journal: Practice and Research, 53(4), 299-237.

Development of New Constructs:

Construct one—reformation ought to commence at the most rudimentary-level, involving students.

Analysis with student-level data allows for account of student mobility.

Gross et al. (2009) reveals that—student-level data provide the opportunity to examine the differential effect of CSR (Comprehensive Student Reform) awards across students of different types (p. 114). In short, the data gathered and tabulated provides direct and pragmatic insights to addressing and responding to the specific needs of pertinent and target student body.

Gross, B., Booker, T.K., & Goldhaber, D. (2009). *Boosting student achievement: The effect of comprehensive school reform on student achievement. Educational Evaluation and Policy Analysis, 31*(2), 111-126.

Information concerning one's social environment is equally important to collective children acquisition.

Akos and Ellis (2008) quoting Comer profess that "research suggests that children from 5 to 8 years old take in information about their own identity and others' differences, whereas children between 8 and 12 years old begin to internalize and act on society's expectations" (1989; p. 26). In short, the results afford keen and vital insights for designing such a system that is anything but a cookie-cutter format.

Akos, P., & Ellis, C.M. (2008). *Racial identity: A case for school counselor individual and systemic intervention. Journal of Counseling and Development, 86*(1), 26-33. 25

Coaching is seen as a collaborative process.

Hart et al. (2001) reveals that "it appears to be an activity that is shared by both parties and not controlled by the coach. The coach will guide the person being coached but will not directly assume responsibility for the outcome" (p. 234). In short, it is safe to 30 presume and thus establish a form understanding of the necessity for a system where information and valuable insights are considered flexible, subject-to-change, and wholly reciprocate in-nature.

Hart, V., Blattner, J., & Leipsic, S. (2001). *Coaching versus therapy: A perspective. Consulting Psychology Journal: Practice and Research, 53*(4), 299-237.

Combination of predictors indicates the highest-levels of efficaciousness.

McCollum and Kajs (2009) assert that the fundamental predictors include:

1. Performance-approach orientation;
2. Mastery-approach orientation;
3. Mastery-avoidance orientation (p. 38).

In short, these same predictors serve to "indicate the highest-levels of efficaciousness for some of the dimensions of efficacy in the SAES" (McCollum & Kajs, 2009, p. 38). Hence, these same predictors identified and germane and vital are to serve as core pillars upon which the comprehensive system is to be established.

McCollum, D.L., Kais, L.T. (2009). *Examining the relationship between school administrators' efficacy and goal orientations. Educational Research Quarterly, 32*(3), 29-46. 20

Importance of open & direct communication—parents, students, and teachers
Auberach (2009) citing Fruchter et al. divulges that "family and community engagement are increasingly seen as powerful tools for making schools more equitable, culturally responsive, and collaborative" (p. 10).
Auberbach, S. (2009). *Walking the walk: Portraits in leadership for family engagement in urban schools. The School Community Journal, 19*(1), 9-31.

Accountability pressures requiring improvement—students, schools, and districts.
Mangin and Stoelinga (2010) assert that "new research should examine the role that other school-level leaders—both formal and informal—and district-level leaders play in creating the organizational structures necessary for effective teacher leadership" (p. 58). In short, in order for such a system of reformation to become effective it requires active participation by all feasible key participators and players.
Mangin, M.M., & Stoelinga, S.R. (2010). *The future of instructional teacher leader roles. The Educational Forum, 74*(1), 49-62.

References:

Akos, P., & Ellis, C.M. (2008). Racial identity: A case for school counselor individual and systemic intervention. *Journal of Counseling and Development, 86*(1), 26-33.

Auberbach, S. (2009). *Walking the walk: Portraits in leadership for family engagement in urban schools. The School Community Journal, 19*(1), 9-31.

Gross, B., Booker, T.K., & Goldhaber, D. (2009). *Boosting student achievement: The effect of comprehensive school reform on student achievement. Educational Evaluation and Policy Analysis, 31*(2), 111-126.

Hart, V., Blattner, J., & Leipsic, S. (2001). *Coaching versus therapy: A perspective. Consulting Psychology Journal: Practice and Research, 53*(4), 299-237.

Mangin, M.M., & Stoelinga, S.R. (2010). *The future of instructional teacher leader roles. The Educational Forum, 74*(1), 49-62.

McCollum, D.L., Kais, L.T. (2009). *Examining the relationship between school administrators' efficacy and goal orientations. Educational Research Quarterly, 32*(3), 29-46.

[Syllabus]

Faculty Bio-sketch:

Hello student, prospective colleague and friend. I am pleased to meet you, in fact, allow me to formally introduce myself for my name is Professor Claude E. Bonet and I am but one of several faculty commissioned to guide you through this "life-transforming" process. I am best summarized as a Perpetual Student of the Transforming Academia. What I mean—core teaching philosophy, is that the underlying purpose for my being here—literally begins and ends at the moment where the highest-caliber of comprehensive-cognitive thinking begins to materialize, in your life.

Anyway, this course is designed upon a novel concept called the Hyper-meta Cognition™® Theoretical Learning Model. It is the plane where the highest-level of consistent, unparalleled critical thinking takes place. Pertinent to my credentials—academic and professional, I have a cumulative of 15+ years—traditional and nontraditional—in the realm of communications, electronics, and computer information technology, which includes both systems and network design-engineering. Also, I possess a vast breadth and depth of knowledge in the disciplines of coaching and mentoring. Currently I possess a Bachelor of Science Degree in Computer Information Systems, as well as Master of Arts Degree; I have successfully completed 4 intense years of doctoral-level academic training at 101 cumulative quarter hours plus 3 residencies.

In closing, again, I am honored and privileged in having this rich opportunity for not only catapulting you to the next-dimension, but likewise learn new, novel, and unique ways of: 1. Communicating; 2. Knowing; 3. Reasoning; 4. Thinking; 5. Understanding, from each one of you—collectively and individually. We wish you lasting success!

What You Can Expect from QCAD1501.E1, the Clay & Pine Phase?

1. That the next step you take will profoundly impact your life as a professional critical thinker;
2. You will be deeply pleased that you decided to enroll, participate, and proceed;
3. Upon completion of this course, you will have unparalleled passion for taking the next two phases;
4. You will connect with like-minded and like-spirited colleagues and friends;
5. If nothing else, you will be equipped for effectuating constructive and lasting change within your corresponding spheres of influence.

What You Can Expect from Professor Claude E Bonet?

1. Nothing less than my absolute best. I am committed to your success;
2. That I am always available to assist you. That is, if time permits, I will respond expeditiously;
3. To be fair and impartial as it relates to facilitating an overall grade and performance report;

4. To provide and thus make available all the critical information, resources, and tools as required for success.

Attendance Policy:

In order to receive full credit, acquire certification, and thus graduate, the student must be present for all scheduled—face-to-face, meetings. Only the most important and urgent excuses are allowed; in the event of an unforeseen circumstance you are afforded a full refund (Refund is @ maximum 75% after 5 day advance-notification expires).

Philanthropic Partnerships/Faculty Commissions:

You're active participation is not only an excellent way to invest in your life. But most importantly, you are literally also transporting healing and restoration to a select part of the world. In short, a total of 20% of the overall enrollment and registration fees is being invested into the following charitable-philanthropic organizations:

1. **SmileTrain**. The website is: http://www.smiletrain.org. Its primary mission is the restoration of lives of children born with a cleft, as well as deformed mouth or palate. Notice, the contribution amount is @ 5%.
2. **The American Cancer Society**. The website is: http://www.cancer.org. Its primary mission is the ongoing fight to find a cure to the cancer epidemic. Notice, the *contribution amount* is 5%.
3. **National Fallen Heroes Foundation**. The website is: http://www.nfhf.org/. Its primary mission is to afford the rightfully due honor and respect for paying the ultimate sacrifice is defense of this great nation. Notice, the *contribution rate* is 5%.
4. **Faculty Shareholder Program**. The primary objective for this is to firstly create a healthy competitive environment where maximum performance and then some is normal. Also, as a reward for unwavering commitment and top performance, each top achiever is richly rewarded. Notice, the *commission scale* is: 1. *Top-place*

faculty@ 3%; 2. *Second-best@* 2.5%; 3. *Third-best@*2.0%; 4. *Fourth-best@*1.5%; 5. *Fifth-best@*1.0%; 6. Everyone else @0.05%. Notice, the percentile wholly depends upon student survey-form feedback.

Residency Premise:

Home—*the place where, when you go there, they have to take you in* (McLellan quoting Frost, 1998, p. 87).

Wisdom—*I was always looking outside myself for strength and confidence but it comes from within. It is there all the time.*—Anna Freud.

Understanding—*he who calls in the aid of an equal understanding doubles his own* (McLellan quoting Burke, Ibid, p. 277).

Counsel—*A pint of example is worth a gallon of advice* (McLellan quoting Anonymous-Author, Ibid, p. 60).

Reference Sources:

McLellan, V. (1998). Wise words and quotes: An intriguing collection of popular quotes by famous people and wise sayings from scripture. Wheaton, IL: Tyndale House Publishers. ISBN: 0842336710.

Wisdom for our time: A Helen exley giftbook. (1999). Spencer, MA: Exley Publications Ltd. ISBN: 1861875142.

Key Term Application:

quan•tum (kwän-təm\) n., pl

1. A quantity or amount;
2. Something that can be counted or measured

3. Physics. a. The smallest amount of a physical quantity that can exist independently, especially a discrete quantity of electromagnetic radiation; b. This amount of energy regarded as a unit.

—attributive. ("The American Heritage Dictionary", p. 1480).

Application to residency:

The overall critical thinking process which occurs within the context of this x-treme residency is similar to the research and development which consistently transpires at a scientific research laboratory. Every interaction in fact between participants, as well as the acquisition and facilitation of novel information are both contained and controlled. However, limitless participation is also highly encouraged. In short, the overall breadth and depth of the information that is facilitated is both a defined and specific amount and quality which is calculated; it is even acutely calibrated and measured.

Reference Source:

The American Heritage Dictionary (3rd ed.). (1994). New York, NY: Dell Publishing. ISBN: 0440219616.
Foundational Concept—The Fusion of Innovation with Execution!

[Structural Dynamics of Comprehensive Residency]

The comprehensive residency is comprised of three fundamental phases:

1. **Phase I is the—Pine & Clay Phase**. In short, it covers nothing more than the bare essential nuts-and-bolts thereof; it is the most rudimentary-elementary of all three phases.
2. **Phase II is the—Stone & Mortar Phase**. In short, it covers the vital intricacies all applicable to a real world context. It is the intermediate stage of critical thinking, of

course acutely germane to change, development, and growth. It literally connects the dots and addresses the direct relevance it has, again, in a real-world context.

3. **Phase III is the—Glass & Metal Phase**. It covers the cosmetics thereof. It approaches critical thinking pertinent to its encompassing accessories thereof. These accessories can also be referred to as the benefits and perks resulting from effective critical thinking. In short, it is the actual phase where every student makes critical thinking their own. It directly correlates to each one's unique set of attributes and personality. It is, again, comprised accordingly: 1. Phase I, aka—Clay & Pine Phase; 2. Phase II, aka—Stone & Mortar Phase; 3. Phase III, aka—Glass & Metal Phase.

Residency Competencies (5 Core):

1. Afford each learner the opportunity to engage in high-impact, aka—x-treme residency critical thinking sessions.
2. Facilitate critical thinking as a discipline and essential activity, in a whole new style, with an innovative and novel approach.
3. Prepare students to become highly competent, highly effective, and highly skilled critical thinkers.
4. Critically examine attributes of highly competent, highly effective, and highly skilled critical thinkers.
5. Assess, calibrate, and redesign (if necessary) the overall change, development, and growth of each student-participant.

Residency Platform:

1. Phase I: Face-to-face Learning Context (Summer 2011).
2. Phase II: Hybrid Learning Context (Winter 2011).
3. Phase III: Online & Remote Learning Context (Summer 2012).

[Residency Technologies]

Expectations Statement:

Quantum Aca(yna^{E3})mics^{SM®}: A Critical Thinking Residency—face-to-face, (hybrid) and online components, is fundamentally established upon a novel and innovative leaning modality thus comprised of three core pillars: 1. Active critical debate and discussion; 2. Active reflective & inflective learning; 3. Unhindered, yet respectful communication. It encompasses teaching—interactive: communicating, learning, reflection, and critical debate, all acutely germane to the Hyper-meta Cognition™® Theoretical Learning Model. Lastly, for more in-depth and detailed information, please refer to official Participator Expectations Sheet. It can be found within detailed information packet; it is provided @ on-site official registration.

Supplemental Expectations (7 Core):

1. Read and be familiar with material—assignments-readings and syllabus.
2. Remain active and fully engaged participants.
3. Seek assistance—mentors (level one), cohorts-peers (level two), and inner-self (level three).
4. Stay on course regarding assessments, assignments, and participation.
5. Challenge cohorts and peers unto higher dimensions of critical thinking and critical reasoning.
6. Be consistently respectful of others—contributions, insights, and opinions.
7. Successfully matriculate in an above-standard manner.

In fact, all active participants—inclusive of faculty and learners, challenge, critique, and make objective recommendations all for the sake of significantly contributing towards the overall lasting and ongoing success of each participant's overall learning experience.

Residency Conduct:

1. Academic Honesty & Integrity.
2. Commitment to Attend Every Session.
3. Respect for Diversity Statement.
4. Commitment to Active & Unrestrained Participation.
5. Invest Nothing Less than Absolute Best Statement.

Residency Materials-Requisite Readings:

[Required] Each student must purchase and thus utilize each and every item—article, book, and supplemental item thereof, as listed towards the successful completion of this residency. In fact, to choose not to utilize the aforementioned items is to actively decide to not successfully matriculate throughout the breadth and length of this learning program. It is assumed and presumed that your enrollment in this learning program is a—statement of unwavering commitment for completing-fulfilling all set requisites applicable to this residency.

In short, it is strongly advised and recommended that each student purchase and utilize each and every listed item.

Articles:

Brookfield, S. (1995). The getting of wisdom: What critically reflective teaching is and why it's important. Retrieved from http://www.nl.edu/academics/cas/ace/faculty papers/ StephenBrookfield_Wisdom.cfm

Brookfield, S. (2006). Discussion as a way of teaching. Retrieved from htttp:// stephenbrookfield.com_Dr._Stephen_D._Brookfield/Workshop_Materials_files/ Discussion_Materials.pdf

Lieb, S. (1991). Principles of adult learning: Adults as learners. Retrieved from http:// wcwts.wisc.edu/mandatedreporter/adult_learning.pdf

Books:

Aamodt, S., & Wang, S. (2008). Welcome to your brain: Why you lose your car keys but never forget how to drive and other puzzles of everyday life. New York, NY: Bloomsbury, USA. ISBN-13: 9781596912830.

Allen, J. (1992). As a man thinketh. New York, NY: Barnes & Noble Publishing, Inc. ISBN-13: 9780760733936.

Katz, L.C., & Rubin, M. (1999). Keep your brain alive: 83 Neurobic exercises to help prevent memory loss and increase mental fitness. New York, NY: Workman Publishing Company. ISBN: 0761110526.

Nee, Watchman. (1972). The latent power of the soul. New York, NY: Christian Fellowship Publishers, Inc. ISBN: 093500825X.

Parlette, R. (1988). The university of hard knocks: Learning to do what winners do. Fort Worth, TX: Brownlow Publishing Company, Inc. ISBN: 0915720051.

Waldrop, L.W. (2006). Becoming an architect: A guide to careers in design. Hoboken, NJ: John Wiley & Sons, Inc. ISBN-10: 0471709549

Web Sites:

Ennis, R.H. (2003-2011). What is critical thinking? Retrieved from http://www.criticalthinking.net/

Residency Learning Assessments (6 Core)

1. Good Practice Audit (faculty & students).
2. Critical Incident Questionnaires (students).
3. Appreciative Inquiry Worksheet (students).
4. Traditional Tests—Multiples Choice, and True/False (students).
5. Anonymous Survey Forms (students & faculty).
6. Workshop Monitors—Assess, Observe, and Measure Performance (faculty).

Pertinent to the Good Practice Audit, it essentially creates a collaborative learning setting in which problems are addressed, discussed, and ultimately resolved. It is "a three phase process in which teachers [and applicable to students] search their experiences for good resources to common problems they encounter" (Brookfield, 1995, p. 161). It also thus comprises an amalgamation or composite of "individual reflection and collaborative critical analysis and is focused on helping people deal with difficulties they have themselves identified" (Ibid). Hence, while engaging therein much needed critical dialogue and critical reflection, the body of participants experience critical reflection, open and candid sharing, and comprehensive reflective analysis. In short, the encompassing process itself consists of three rudimentary phases: 1. Problem formulation; 2. Individual and collective analysis; 3. Compilation of suggestions for practice. Notice, even though the GPA was initially intended for educators and teachers, it can likewise—through slight recalibration, be utilized for its participating residency-students.

Pertinent to the Critical Incident Questionnaire, it "helps us to embed our teaching in accurate information about students'learning that is regularly solicited and anonymously given" (Brookfield, 1995, p. 114). The structural layout of the questionnaire exists as "a single page form that is handed out to students at the end of the last class", it includes five simple and straight forward questions "each of which asks students to write down some details about events that happened in the class" during that corresponding week of activity (Brookfield, 1995, p. 114).

Hence, a brief list of its relevant questions includes:

1. At what moment did you feel most engaged within the context of what was taking place within the session/room?
2. At what moment did you feel most distanced from what was taking place within the session-room?
3. What action that anyone took in the class this week did you find most alarming and helpful?

4. What action that anyone took in the class this week did you find most puzzling or confusing?

5. What specific key points do you find most applicable to your current working sphere of influence?

6. What specific recommendation would you make and thus submit for the sake of improving the overall quality of the workshop learning experience?

7. In comparison to the person you were on day one of the workshop, what fundamental changes

In short, the most important benefit of participating in the Critical Incident Questionnaire is that the fundamental dynamics of the learning program can be addressed, confronted, and ultimately, if considered of urgent necessity, revised, reinvented, or reconstructed all for the sake of becoming a more effective learning experience.

Pertinent to the Appreciative Inquiry Worksheet, it exists with the primary purpose for engaging in "an ongoing process for investigating and understanding critical 15 organization issues", it provokes and stimulates: 1. Organization members' interest and ability in exploring critical issues using evaluation logic; 2. Organization members' involvement in evaluative processes, and; 3. The personal and professional growth of individuals within the organization (Preskill & Catsambas, 2006, p. 39). It also focuses thereon its evaluators being equipped in assessing and documenting students involvement 20 and performance; specifically it addresses and—responds to the evolving requirements of those who duct evaluations (Ibid, p. 41). Hence, it ensures that its team of evaluators-monitors are provided—a direction for the evaluation that was more constructive than it might have been had another process been used (Ibid, p. 73).

Next, the main goals of the Appreciative Inquiry Worksheet are to address and 25 thus actively concentrate thereon two rudimentary components of the comprehensive evaluative process: 1. The 4-D Model; 2. The 4-I Model. As discussed in one of the previous paragraphs, the 4-D Model includes the following four phases; 1. Discovery; 2. Dreaming; 3 Designing; 4. Destiny.

Whereas, the 4-I Model includes the following four phases: 1. Inquire; 2. Imagine; 3. Innovate; 4. Implement (Preskill, 2006, p. 8, slide 10). 30 In short, the underlying-main benefit of utilizing the Appreciative Inquiry Worksheet is to essentially—add to existing evaluation systems, or develop new evaluation systems (Ibid, p. 15, slide 30).

[Grading Statistics]

Activity: Weight Scoring Guide

1. Debate-Participation 60% Debate-Participation Scoring Guide
    -critical acumen (initial) @ 7%
    -critical acumen (growth and improvement) @ 13%
    -authentic wit (initial) @ 7%
    -authentic wit (growth and improvement) @ 13%
    -humor & charisma-application (initial) @ 7%
    -humor & charisma-application (growth & improvement @ 13%
    Total scoring @ 60%

2. Assessment & Tests 40% Assessment & Tests Scoring Guide
    Notice: all tests and assessments are completed on day #2, and day #5.
    -Good Practice Audit (day 2) @ 3%
    -Good Practice Audit (day 5) @ 7%
    -Critical Incident Questionnaires (day 2) @ 3%
    -Critical Incident Questionnaires (day 5) @ 7%
    -Appreciative Inquiry Worksheet (day 2) @ 3%
    -Appreciative Inquiry Worksheet (day 2) @ 7%
    -Traditional Tests-MC, T/F (day 5) @ 10%
    Total scoring @ 40%

Final Course Grade Scale:

A = 95-100%
B = 90-94.9%

C = 85-89.9%

D = 80-84.9% 30

F = ≤ 79.9

Residency Dates & Daily Itinerary

Commences: Wednesday, June 6, 2014

Expires: Sunday, June 10, 2014

Notice: A detailed information packet will be provided upon on-site official registration. Please refer to information table. Onsite staff and faculty-instructors are there to assist you. If there are any questions or issues which need immediate response, please do not hesitate. We are excited and privileged that you decided to participate and become actively engaged. We believe 5 the best to be acquired and thus taken away from this overall learning experience!

Residency Outline Overview:

Unit 1—Exactly Why Am I Participating: Underlying Motivations?

Unit 1 Introduction 10

Welcome to Quantum Acad(yna^{E3})mics$^{SM®}$: A Critical Thinking Residency. This residency has be designed and developed in order to afford each student the opportunity to develop and strengthen their core critical thinking muscles. It is designed and intended for all individuals—college, university, and graduate-level, whom are interested in not only understanding what critical thinking is, but most importantly how to develop, and eventually become a—Master of Hyper-meta cognition.

As a result, the individual will be equipped in greatly improving their corresponding spheres of influence. We are most confident that you will become nothing less than highly competent, highly effective, and highly skilled agents of constructive & lasting change.

Anyhow, regarding unit one, the underlying objective is to gain full insights and 20 understandings into the intricacies & motivations behind taking this residency. That is, whether it involves simply understanding what critical thinking is and all that it entails, or merely to develop the knowledge that one already possesses and thus progress towards the next-level of personal mastery. One thing is certain you will gain a broader and deeper, as well as a richer understanding into not only critical thinking as a concept, but most importantly as an opportunity 25 for greatly impacting one's spheres of influence. We wish you much success!!!

Unit 1 Objectives (3 Core Takeaways)

To successfully complete the first unit, the student must acquire the basic essentials of critical thinking:

1. Critically assess, examine, and investigate one's underlying motivations—personal and professional.
2. Identify and critically discuss the importance and relevance of this unit to the real-world.
3. Assess the definition of wisdom and make it applicable to one's individual context.

Engaging the Next Generation of Faculty

Fundamental Article Argument:

The chief argumentative hypothesis involves the concern, as well as the apprehension as to whether or not the forthcoming generations of faculty—educational leaders are suffice prepared for actively engaging in the comprehensive scope of the academic process. Perhaps the most appropriate question is, have we been diligent in exhausting all of the necessities for invoking the passion of the next generation for becoming actively engaged in impacting their world?

According to David Maxwell, in fact, a caucus involving 18 college and university presidents convened in which—there was a worried discussion about the perception that younger faculty currently entering the professoriate are increasingly less engaged in the affairs of their institution, in fulfilling their responsibilities inherent in the model of shared governance, and in assuming these roles that will prepare them for institutional leadership (2009, p. 5). The only lasting reality is, nevertheless, that the next generation of faculty can; yes, it will be suffice equipped only if we annex the next impending moment and thus assist and afford them all of the tools and resources needed for not only actively engaging in the relevant due process, but rather addressing and resolving any issue, hence crisis, that has yet to arise. In short, it is a list of tools-resources all inclusive of the following: the knowledge and the wisdom; the passion and the vision, all requisites for transforming into a highly effective and highly influential legion-militia of next generation academics leaders.

Reason for the Research:

The chief reason or rationale behind the research is to afford leaders whom did not initially participate in the roundtable discussion—the spring 2007 convention, pragmatic insights into the results or findings thereof. In other words, David Maxwell deemed it his avowed duty as well as devoted responsibility for awakening the collective academic consciousness and thus sounding forth the clarion call for intrinsic transformation; it is a transformation of both paradigms as well as modalities. It is such a resounding call, in fact, that set forth a chain reaction requiring immediate action in engaging the core concerns at hand. For example, Mr. Maxwell acutely insinuates that the relevant issues are in fact quite antiquated in nature; it is a perpetual progress that finds its origin multiplied generations ago.

Moreover, he asserts,—It may look like an uphill struggle: National surveys of college and university faculty for decades have consistently indicated that faculty member's loyalties are typically first to their discipline, second to their department, and only third to the institution in which they are employed (Maxwell, 2009, p. 6). The author identifies the aforementioned as the fundamental pillar upon which all other concerns or issues are constructed thereupon.

In regards to focusing thereon the solution rather than the problem Mr. Maxwell submits a brief list of recommendations, inclusive of the following: i. listen to the young faculty; ii. ensure that every one of them has a senior mentor; iii. help them connect their passions to the missions and goals of the institution; iv. create an institutional development program that prepares them for the broad range of leadership roles; v. create administrative internships for younger faculty (2009, p. 6).

Accordingly, David Maxwell affirms that it is ultimately our obligation; yes, it is our 10 responsibility in equipping and thus provoking the next generation of faculty for becoming active participators in the fashioning-shaping of their future reality of higher academic matriculation. In short, Maxwell asserts, "We want them to help us form an institution that can respond to demands of a future that we cannot yet see very clearly" (p. 7).

Research Questions: For starters, it is imperative to mention that the research findings do not include explicit or direct questions. Rather the research questions, on the contrary, are quite implicitly embedded within the intricacies of the article itself. The questions in fact have intentionally been formulated in such a way as to invite and awaken, hence arouse the necessary critical thinking faculties all necessary for addressing and resolving the aforementioned challenges set before; the chief motivation is to incite a domino effect of the targeted readers to likewise become actively engaged participators.

In short, it is a movement that must solicit active change agents from all quadrants of the panoramic academic sphere, inclusive of both current faculty-academic leaders and the next generation of faculty-academic leaders. With that said, the identifiable questions are: i. Have we set such an example as to encourage the next generation of faculty for becoming actively engaged; ii. What issues or challenges must be addressed before we can progress further; iii. Who are the participators-active and inactive; iv. What steps must be implemented or engaged in resolving the challenges set before; v. What fail safe mechanism or contingency plan must be engineered, just in case the preferential options fall dire short.

In regards to the first question, it is found within the context particles of the article title, *Engaging the Next Generation of Faculty*. In other words, the question initially was arisen by the challenge or alarm being activated from the onset. After all, in a nutshell, it boils down to the fundamental premise upon which why the author constructed the article in the first. In regards to the second question, it is embedded within the context of page five, in which the author lists the aforementioned core concerns addressed at the spring 2007 roundtable discussion. In regards to the third question, it is found embedded within the intricacies of the first paragraph, entitled "Generation-Why". Eventhough, the author's main focus is upon the next generation of faculty, it is imperative that a panoramic frame of reference be kept at the forefront of one's own consciousness. In other words, the issues or challenges cannot be resolved without suffice including the current faculty-leaders, the institution executive staff and president, and the collective culture at-large. In regards to the fourth and fifth questions, it is embedded within the—list of recommendations detailed by the author.

These recommendations, in fact, include pragmatic strategies which ought to be utilized in ensuring that a viable environment is created, which ultimately results in the overall objective becoming fully realized. The ultimate objective in short involves unleashing a next generation of faculty who are not only effective in reaching their generating, rather actively engaged in fashioning their future of higher academic matriculation and maturation.

Hypothesis:

The hypothesis or fundamental claim is that the current regime of academic leadership has fallen short in mentoring or rising up a next generation of faculty whom are actively engaged in the comprehensive scope of academic matriculation; the null hypothesis is: $\mu GY \leq 0$ or the p-20 value is greater than (>) the assumed default significance-level of $= 0.05$. David Maxwell thus conceded, "there seems to be a growing body of convincing evidence that something indeed is different, and there are several factors that may explain the difference" (2009, p. 6). Consequently, the next generation of faculty-academia has fallen dire short of exceeding and thus existing well beyond the standard means parameter, all within the comprehensive academic participative process!

Type and Methodology of Research:

In regards to the dilemma involving whether or not a direct linear correlation exits between the research article and the collective realm of Statistics, in particularly this course, the answer is a resounding yes! Similarly, there are in fact several chief statistical techniques that are not only embedded within the text, but more importantly have been utilized within previous coursework sessions thus far. The list of techniques is accordingly: i. Hypothesis Testing Claim Fundamentals; ii. The P-Value Method; iii. Type I and Type II Errors; iv. and, Inferences from Matched Pairs.

In regards to the first technique, Hypothesis Testing Claim Fundamentals, it is quite apparent that the set pair of requirements, required for the testing to become engaged, do exist; the requirements are called the null hypothesis (denoted as Ho) and the alternative hypothesis (denoted as H1 or Ha) accordingly. According to Mario Triola, the null hypothesis is—a statement that the value of a population parameter (such as proportion, mean, or standard deviation) is equal to some claimed value (2007, p. 413). Triola defines on the other hand that the alternative hypothesis is—the statement that the parameter has a value that somehow differs from the null hypothesis (p. 414). In brief, it is best correlated or identified as being that of the initial or original claim. In regards to the second technique, The P-Value Method, it is defined as the—probability of getting a value of the test statistic that is at least as extreme as the one representing the sample data, assuming that the null hypothesis is true (Triola, 2007, p. 418).

Nonetheless, in regards to the intricacies or correlation of listed technique to the research article, there exist both single and multiple proportions. For example, Maxwell concedes that "It is not easy to quantify objectively the fact that this phenomenon of faculty disengagement from the institutional governance is increasing, other than the fact that membership in the American Association of University Professors is less than half

(< 0.50 %) of what it was in 1970)" (2009, p. 6)). He continues (assumed direct linear correlation to the original claim, alternative hypothesis), "But there seems to be a growing body of convincing evidence that something indeed is different, and there are several factors that may explain the difference" (p. 6). In brief, this is but a solitary illustration of the listed correlating probability elements embedded within the article textual context. Lastly, in regards to the remaining techniques, for the sake of verbiage restraints as well as contextual convenience, they will remain as but mere shadowy examples, both of which lack substantive illustrative information relevancy.

Results:

After engaging in a thoroughly extrapolative process, the author arrives at the following final conclusions. The final conclusions are in fact directly correlated to the listed recommendations for resolving the identified chief issue. Before delving into the listed conclusions, however, it is imperative to first re-examine or reassess the chief problem, as actively prognosticated by David Maxwell. Thus, the chief problem, again, involves the "worried 30 discussion about the perception that younger faculty currently entering the professoriate are increasingly less engaged in the affairs of their institution, in fulfilling their responsibilities inherent in the model of shared governance, and in assuming these roles that will prepare them for institutional leadership" (2009, p. 5). Or in regards to the *original hypothesis claim*: H1(alternative hypothesis), the current regime of academic leadership has fallen short in mentoring or rising up a next generation of faculty whom are actively engaged in the comprehensive scope of academic matriculation. In short, the conclusion's ultimate objective is not only to afford recommendations, but rather bridge the gap between both the mistakes and shortcomings of old, and henceforth the reformation or the reinvention of highly efficient and novel strategies-techniques.

Effective leadership techniques or modalities that will in due course both equip and thus prove the next generation of faculty for becoming active participators in the fashioning of their future reality of higher academic matriculation-maturation. In summary, the concluding research findings involve the followings dynamics. The first dynamic involves an open and candid communication between the current regime of leadership-academia, as well as the targeted next generation thereof. The second dynamic involves the active participation, hence embracing of the comprehensive scope of the academic process. In brief, the next generation will—recognize—and embrace—the fact that the future of the institution in many important ways looks more like them than it does like those of us who have been around for awhile (Maxwell, 2009, p. 7). As a direct result, the third dynamic will thus become activated and unleashed; the third dynamic involves the awakening or necessary passion for becoming actively engaged in shaping "an institution that is responsive to the needs and aspirations of generations of students who have not yet been born" (2009, p. 7). Lastly, the fourth dynamic ultimately involves the next generation inheriting a model that is not only pragmatically relevant, rather one in which they had a direct supporting role in developing, hence bring forth into reality.

Research Conclusion:

The research conclusion includes the following predetermined questions, accordingly: i. Was there information that the author omitted that you felt should have been included; ii. In your opinion were there methodical flaws; iii. Did anything surprise you; iv. Did you learn anything significant through this review process; v. How would you grade this research and why; vi. and lastly, "Would you be proud to have your name on this research as a co-author?" In regards to the question one, information was omitted and thus should have been galvanized—directly and indirectly, from the target audience base. In other words, the audience should have included any of the following: i. Students-from an intrinsic, hence prospective leadership perspective; ii. Students-from an explicit, hence non-leadership prospective perspective; iii. Individuals remote from the sphere of academics yet are directly influenced by the realm of leadership; v. Current Leaders existing outside the sphere of direct academics. Thus, if any of the listed individuals would have been included it would have indubitably afforded a panoramic perspective for leadership, past, present, and the imminent future.

As a direct result, this will suffice and thoroughly equip not only the next generation, but also the current academic regime with all of the tools and resources necessary for effectuating lasting positive chance. In regards to question two, concerning methodical flaws, the only feasible answer is the lack of providing a panoramic-360 degree approach, all necessary in my opinion for effectively approaching the core issues as hand. In brief, the structure of the research involves more concentration of the present, which ultimately results in but a limited, one-dimensional vantage point. In regards to the question three, no, I was neither alarmed nor surprised by anything listed-mentioned within the context of the text. The primary reason for this is because, in short, it is something that I expect or have repeatedly experienced coming forth from the previous generational paradigm. In other words, as many are fairly well astute, the previous generation have consistently resolved issues, hence addressed otherwise overwhelming crisis through the utilization of a linear, one-dimensional method of approach. Thus, this limits the reader for arriving at a complete and thorough understanding of every feasible problem-solution dimension.

In regards to questions four and five, the main thing in which I can carry away from the research and henceforth implement into mine own sphere of influence is a greater appreciation for the vital necessity in ensuring that we haste no more in addressing the chief issues at hand.

After all, if we fail to address the issues and rather elect to travel the road less occupied, the world in which we live will ultimately cease and desist. Concerning the second part of the same question, conclusively I would grade the research, with a scale of one to ten, as an eight (8). The primary reason for this is because the author failed to effectively tie up the loose ends. These—loose ends includes not only the aforementioned questions one through three, but rather a deep correlation between the issues of before, the issues at hand, and the imminent future, comprised of both issues that have yet to arise and likewise the corresponding solutions thereof.

Lastly, in regards to the sixth and final question, I can honestly assert that I indeed will, at least at the onset, be quite apprehensive in including my name as a co-author for David Maxwell's research. On the other hand, I am not at all removing myself entirely from any possibility of ever being included therein. The only enduring concern is the necessity for including all of the before listed recommendations that have been omitted, and yet are still highly advised. Only after this process has become fully engaged, will I perhaps thoughtfully reconsider the submission, the accepting thereof any invitation in becoming an active participator, a research project co-author.

Abstract:

The Adult Learner Assessment (ALA) is an instrument and tool that measures the current level of understanding in which students have navigated and thus matriculated there into. ALA "helps individual college teachers obtain useful feedback on what, how much, and how well their students are learning:" (Angelo & Cross, 1993, p. 3). If facilitated effectively, the inevitable result will be the enhanced "effectiveness of many of these decisions by providing more objective information on which to base judgments" (Gronlund & Waugh, 2009, p. 4).

Pertinent to its fundamental purpose, it affords both the author and readers alike the opportunity to assess and construct a most necessary learning assessment infrastructure. Hence, the underlying purpose is to construct a theoretically pragmatic framework upon which sound understanding is established and erected thereon. It allows the diverse parties germane to the assessment discuss the overarching concept, as well as the drafting and identification of a threshold-line which ultimately distinguishes the fusion point between the theoretical foundation, as well as the application within a real-world context.

Relevant to the detailed and systematic correlation existing between instruction and the facilitation of diverse assessments. Moreover, both actually "require that we clearly specify the learning outcomes to be achieved by students, and the provisions of well-designed assessments closely parallel the characteristics of effective instruction" (Gronlund & Waugh, 2009, p. 3). The collective project is sub-divided into three core components; they include: 1. Unit 2—ALA Introduction Draft; Unit 5—ALA Assessment Section Draft; 2. Unit 7—Interpretation of Results Draft; 3. Unit 10—ALA Comprehensive-Final

Project, collectively. In a summative nutshell, the main residency-course objective—at the concluding phase or checkpoint—is that the active engager will wholly and successfully develop a summative assessment, appropriate for the full utilization by the germane body of adult student learners.

ALA Introduction Draft:

The name of the first section is the ALA Introduction Draft. This section is comprised of the following vital components: 1. Defining the assessment's type and nature; 2. Identifying and explaining the hypothetical learner; 3. Identifying the target learning populations; 4. Identifying at least three learning outcomes to be measured.

Type and Nature of Assessment:

The overarching category-type under which the assessment is identified is called Authentic Assessments. This specific type measures students' current level of understanding, as well as the relevance to resolving real world challenges and issues. It concentrates on "real-life tasks"; it also "stresses the importance of focusing on the application of understandings and skills" (Gronlund & Waugh, 2009, p 2) applicable to pragmatic contextual situations. It is considered a most effective way to determine if students are prepared to function and navigate within the real world.

Identify & Explain the Hypothetical Learner—Target Population:

The hypothetical learner includes students within the age range of eighteen to thirty-five, aka *Generation-Y*, and *The Millenials*. These students possess educational experience ranging from right out of high school up to and including graduate-level studies. They originate from diverse socio-cultural, economic, and religious backgrounds. The economic-statuses include part-time status, full-time status; entrepreneurial status plus self-made millionaires. In short, this is a collective group assembled under the chief principle entitled holistic quasi-cultural engagement.

Identify the Hypothetical Subject:

The hypothetical subject is called Critical Thinking. It is an academic discipline which typically falls under the collective field of Professional and Human Development. It is established upon the core teaching philosophy which affirms that if students are gathered together from vastly diverse parts of the globe, the probability for next-dimension critical thinking is greatly enhanced and increased. As a direct result, the collective student bodies consequentially matriculates into a distinct class of effective and matured analytical-critical thinkers. It is, in short, a novel theoretical framework called Quantum Acad(yna^{E3})mics$^{SM®}$, a three-phased residency which concentrates upon the collective fusing together of innovation and active execution.

Identification of the Core Learning Objectives:

The first objective, Unit 1—Exactly Why Am I Participating—Underlying Motivations, is comprised of three instructional learning tenets:

1. Critically assess, examine, and investigate one's underlying motivations—personal and professional.
2. Identify and critically discuss the importance, as well as its relevance to the real-world.
3. Assess the definition of wisdom, and make it applicable to one's individual context.

The second objective, Unit 2—What is Critical Thinking—Fundamental Intricacies, is comprised of *four instructional tenets*:

1. Grasp firm understanding of the basics of the brain and cognitive functioning.
2. Understand the direct correlation between mastering one's brain and becoming an effective critical thinker.

3. Be able to skillfully and successfully discuss the quasi-dimensional facets of this subject.

4. Develop a balanced and effective argument. Attempt to persuade others pertinent to one's philosophy & novel viewpoint.

In short, if any student is to navigate and matriculate through residency, he or she must first both acquire and master the critical thinking rudimentary.

ALA Section Draft:

The second section is called the ALA Section Draft. The section's main purpose is to afford all parties involved the opportunity to critically assess the intricacies of the actual testing assessment instrument. It includes directions intended for the corresponding administers, plus those taking the assessment; it is comprised of the following sub-sections:

1. It ss divided into two fundamental parts, requires the description of the course, and the design of the actual assessment instrument; it is developed for utilization within the final course project.

2. Section two requires the allocation or provision of directions for both the assessment administrator, as well as the target students engaged in the assessment.

3. Section three requires a description regarding how special needs students will be accommodated.

4. Section four requires the design of the assessment items that are linked to the learning objectives.

5. Section five requires that the assessment item types being matched to the skills being assessed.

6. Section six requires that the design of the assessment consistent regarding the specific context of the learning environment in which it is applicable.

Brief Course Description:

This course is designed and engineered upon an overarching concept dubbed by the author as the Hyper-meta Cognition™® Theoretical Learning Model it is the plane of critical and analytical thinking where the next-dimension of progressive critical analysis-thinking transpires. The chief premise upon which the residency concept is established is that it is the highest-level of consistently unparalleled critical facilitates thereon. It is a next-dimension realm of critical thinking, where the following *two distinct aspects*: 1. Ongoing critical thinking; 2. Intuitive critical reflection, are both fused together. The official name of this course is QCAD 1501.E1, the "Clay & Pine" Phase; it is fundamentally comprised of the following two core components:

1. Unit 1—Exactly Why Am I Participating: Underlying Motivations?
2. Unit 2—What is Critical Thinking: Fundamental Intricacies?

The first unit's learning objective affords deeper insights into the undergirding motivations behind the student enrolling in this residency. The second unit's learning objective involves acquiring the basic essentials of critical thinking. In short, at the conclusion of this residency, the student will have participated in real-world case scenarios, created-applied solution plans, demonstrated mastery of learning program intricacies, and effectively presented and defended applicable arguments.

Learning Environment & Accommodating Special Need Students:

The critical thinking process which occurs within the context of this residency is similar to the research and development prevalent within most scientific research laboratories; every interaction is contained and controlled. The facilitation of information is described as a "face-to-face" learning contextual setting. Pertinent to accommodating students with special needs, the assessment administrators are required to afford as much accommodation as possible. This also includes the extension of required taking time, the assistance in receiving the requisite resources-tools and logistics relevant to taking the assessment.

In short, it involves the necessary finishing of the assessment, as well as the ultimate departures from the premises.

Instructions for the Testing Administrator:

Each question is categorized under the specific unit in which it applies, as identified within the corresponding brackets. The specific unit in which the question or item applies can be found with brackets. Before commencing, the administrator is required to facilitate instructions, as well as remain available for questions which might arise during the session.

ALA Interpretation of Results Draft:

The third and final section is called the ALA Interpretation of Results Draft. The main purpose for this section is to provide insights into the utilization and measuring thereof, germane to the performance-level of students-learners. Hence, these assessments "help individual college teachers obtain useful feedback on what, how much, and how well their students are learning" (Angelo & Cross, 1993, p. 3). Assessments assist educators in shifting the direction of their teaching; serving "to help students make their learning more efficient" (Angelo & Cross, 1993, p. 3). Through the administration of diverse principles-practices, greater contribution is afforded to "more effective classroom instruction and improved student learning" (Gronlund & Waugh, 2009, p. v). It is an integral part of the comprehensive teaching-learning process.

Development of the Assessment and Utilization:

The overarching assessment type of this assignment is the authentic assessment. The authentic assessment is a title for performance assessments that stresses the importance of focusing on the application of understanding and skills to real problems in "real world contextual settings" (Gronlund & Waugh, 2009, p. 2). Regarding both the actual assessment sub-types, and tabulated results, it is triple-tiered. At the course's onset, students are provided a placement assessment; it determines entry-level performance. It addresses a "singular area of concentration": 1. Readiness concern—at the course onset, do the students possess the basic or requisite rudimentary skills? After the course has begun, students are tested in a manner reflective of the formative assessment. This type monitors learning progress. Towards the course's conclusion, students are administered a summative assessment. This type, in fact, is utilized "to determine terminal performance" (Gronlund & Waugh, 2009, pp. 9-10). The next step involves the implementation of fundamental core components; it is divided into four main categories. The actual structural layout is sub-divided into three core sub-sections: 1. True/False; 2. Multiple Choice; 3. Essay Questions. The comprehensive assessment is an assignment draft that assesses, and measures: 1. Aptitude; 2. Performance-level, and; 3. Overall understanding. The chief purpose thereof is to tabulate the target student body's understanding pertinent to the underlying motivation for enrolling in the course, and the subsequent active participating. It delves into the vital insights of the fundamental intricacies of critical thinking; how to tap into and unleash dormant abilities, and the direct application, as well as relevance within a real world context.

This name of the course is QCAD 1501.E1, the "Clay & Pine" Phase. It is designed and engineered upon the overarching concept dubbed as the Hyper-meta Cognition$^{SM®}$ Theoretical Learning Model. The course's chief premise is that there is such a realm in which the highest-level of critical functioning, reasoning, and thinking occurs therein. It is a next-dimension realm of critical thinking, where the following two distinct aspects: 1. Ongoing critical thinking; 2. Intuitive critical reflection, are synergistically fused together.

Interpretation and Grading of Assessment:

Professors Gronlund and Waugh (2009) affirm that the "main purpose of a classroom assessment plan is to improve student learning" (p. 19). The most effective testing assessments are facilitated in the following sequential order: 1. Instruction; 2. Achievement Domain; 3. Achievement Assessment (Gronlund & Waugh, 2009, p. 21). It provides: 1. Relative ranking of students; 2. Description of the learning tasks a student can and cannot perform (Gronlund & Waugh, 2009, p. 24). Concerning the motivation for finding the right assessment, it literally begins and ends at the point in which students are equipped for becoming capable, competent, and effective individuals. Angelo and Cross (1993) divulge that "helping students learn the subject matter of their courses is the most common goal of college teachers, and virtually all teachers try to measure what students are learning about the content being taught" (p. 106).

There are two basic methods for assessment interpretation, the norm-referenced assessment type, and the criterion-referenced assessment type. The specific type utilized in this context is criterion-referenced. Both teachers and students are afforded snapshots into the motivation behind student involvement, as well as sound understanding of the core critical thinking intricacies. The faculty and student body will master the essentials for tapping into and unleashing the set of dormant abilities—critical thinking powers within, as well as identifying a clear link between critical thinking as a concept-discipline and its pragmatic relevance. All of which directly corresponds to the application within a real world situational context. Regarding the chief basis for grading, it is of the absolute grading style. That is "letter grades are typically assigned by comparing a student's performance to a prespecified standard of performance"; it is a common type of grading system that "utilizes letter grades defined by a 100-point system" (Gronlund & Waugh, 2009, p. 192). It is the preferred method of traditional learning institutions.

Assessment Grading Instrument-Rubric:

The main objective for the grading rubric is to assess the student's foundational mastery of the course, as well as the conceptual context. The measured rubric elements are classified into "seven rudimentary categories". The *grading rubric categories* addressed, includes:

1. Efficacy of APA Format-Style;
2. Organization of Ideas and Thoughts;
3. Breadth and Depth of Ideas and Insights;
4. Ability to identify and articulate relevance to real world context;
5. Stability of foundation via mechanical and sentence structure.

6. Multiple Choice Questions;

7. True/False Questions.

The overall purpose for the rubric is the utilization towards to the guiding and navigation throughout the comprehensive assessment process. It directly responds to the questions, such as: 1. Have the course objectives have been mastered; 2. What specific degree of supplemental training is deemed warranted. The rubric is facilitated on three different occasions during each corresponding training course-workshop. The overall content of the course correlates directly to the specific assessment being facilitated.

The rubric's overall quality is considered valid and reliable. The chief justification as to why the rubric is considered as valid is because the results "provide a representative and relevant measure of the achievement domain under consideration" (Gronlund & Waugh, 2009, p. 46). In direct response to why the rubric is considered, thus deemed reliable, it is because regardless of how many times it is taken, consistency in the overall official results tabulated occurs. Professors Oermann & Gaberson (2009) confirm that "scoring rubrics work well for assessing papers" (p. 235).

The assessment rubric assesses and validates the following unit components:

1. Why Am I Participating: Underlying Motivations;

2. What is Critical Thinking: Fundamental Intricacies;

3. Diving Right In, Becoming Actively Engaged;

4. Application of Course Knowledge in Real World Context: How Will I Benefit & Measured Development.

In short, regardless of the frequency of assessment facilitation, plus the utilization of diverse yet equal sample items, the results are consistent.

Conclusion and Final Reflections:

The Adult Learner Assessment (ALA) is an instrument or tool that measures the current level of understanding in which students have navigated and thus matriculated into. The collective ALA project is sub-divided into three core components. The overarching category-type under which the assessment is identified is called Authentic Assessments; it measures students' current level of understanding, as well as the relevance to resolving real world challenges and issues.

The hypothetical learner includes students within the age range of eighteen to thirty-five, aka *Generation-Y*, and *The Millenials*. The name of the hypothetical subject is Critical Thinking; it is an academic discipline which categorized under collective field called Professional and Human Development. Pertinent to the core learning objectives, there are two: 1. Unit 1—Exactly Why Am I Participating—Underlying Motivations; 2. Unit 2—What is Critical Thinking—Fundamental Intricacies. The name of the second section is the Section Draft. The section's main purpose is to afford all parties involved the opportunity to critically assess the intricacies of the actual testing assessment instrument. The collective residency-course is designed and engineered upon a concept referred to as the Hyper-meta Cognition^{SM®} Theoretical Learning Model, the plane in which next-dimension of progressive critical analysis-thinking transpires.

The critical thinking process which occurs is similar to the research and development prevalent within a vast majority of scientific research laboratories. Each question is categorized under the specific unit in which it applies, as identified within a corresponding set of brackets. Learning assessments are used to test and measure the performance-level of students-learners. The overarching assessment type of this comprehensive final project is aptly named the Authentic Assessment. There are two basic methods for assessment interpretation, the *norm-referenced assessment type*, and the *criterion-referenced assessment type*.

Regarding the chief basis for grading, it is of the absolute grading style. In closing, the main objective for the grading rubric is to assess the student's foundational mastery of the course, as well as the conceptual context. The rubric's overall quality is considered valid and reliable. Thus, regardless of the frequency of assessment facilitation, as well as the utilization of diverse yet equal sample items, the results are consistent and unwavering.

Lastly, for the sake of addressing and thus responding to the *key final question*, how the process of interpreting assessments can have an impact on your teaching, the summative-response is as follows. If nothing else, for starters, the individual(s) will be better equipped at interpreting learning-teaching assessments. That is a firm, sound, and unwavering foundational understanding will be thoroughly established. Fisher and Frey (2007) citing Lapp et al. reveals that the following four reasons tests and assessments are commonly used:

1. Diagnosing individual student needs;
2. Informing instruction;
3. Evaluating programs;
4. Providing accountability information (2001, p. 7; p. 100).

In other words, it affords the corresponding parties the necessary information—resources and tools "for drafting and thus facilitation a vitally essential assessing framework which 'provides the roadmap' for the integration of face-to-face and online activities" (Garrison and Vaughan, 2008, p. 3). The underlying point is that it firmly sets and establishes the necessary learning-teaching assessment infrastructure upon which the official measuring and gathering of otherwise vital information derived from vastly diverse cultures and backgrounds can be accomplished.

Thus, a blended community of learning-teaching inquiry can successfully and wholly be completed, from start to finish; it is through and most comprehensive. Hence, the ability to interpret learning-teaching assessments, it positions-postures the applicable assessment team with the chief purpose of engaging therein the "process of gathering information from multiple sources and indicators to make judgments about student learning, achievement, progress, and performance" (Branche et al. citing Frey, 2007, p. 23).

In short, the assessment administrator or facilitator is thoroughly equipped in assessing, measuring, and tabulating the overall ability and competence—past and present—of the target and germane student body to the results, as well as seceding actions thereof, whom will otherwise benefit, regardless of positively or negatively

References:

Angelo, T.A., & Cross, K.P. (1993). *Classroom assessment techniques: A handbook for college teachers.* (2nd ed.). San Francisco, CA: John Wiley & Sons, Inc.

Branche, J., Mullennix, J., & Cohn, E.R. (2007). *Diversity across the curriculum: A guide for faculty in higher education.* San Francisco, CA: Jossey-Bass.

Brookfield, S.D. (1995). *Becoming a critically reflective teacher.* San Francisco, CA: Jossey—Bass.

Brookfield, S.D. (1987). *Developing critical thinkers: Challenge adults to explore alternative ways of thinking and acting.* San Francisco, CA: Jossey-Bass Publishers.

Garrison, D.R., & Vaughan, N.D. (2007). *Blended learning in higher education: Framework, principles, and guidelines.* San Francisco, CA: Jossey-Bass.

Gronlund, N.E., & Waugh, C.K. (2009). *Assessment of student achievement.* (9th ed.). Upper Saddle River, NJ: Pearson-Merrill.

Oermann, M.H., & Gaberson, K.B. (2009). *Evaluation and testing in nursing education.* (3rd ed.). New York, NY: Springer.

Paul, R., & Elder, L. (2006). *Critical thinking: Tools for taking charge of your learning and your life.* (2nd ed.). Upper Saddle River, NJ: Pearson-Prentice Hall.

The Jossey-Bass Reader. (2007). *Educational leadership.* (2nd ed.). San Francisco, CA: John Wiley & Sons, Inc.

Appendix 'A'

Instructions for the Students:

Students are required to thoroughly read the specific directions which correlates to the sub-section. If any questions or issue of concern arises, the student is encouraged to notify any one of the listed and designated test facilitators present during the administration of the assessment test.

Assessment Instrument:

The following assessment test is intended to critically assess, as well as evaluate—measure and tabulate—the target body of students understanding of the underlying motivation for their enrolling in the course, the fundamental intricacies of critical thinking, how to tap into and unleash dormant abilities, and the direct application plus relevance into a real world context.

Target-Subject Population:

Generation 'Y' (Gen-Y), aka *The Millenials*. These are students that fall within the age range of 18 thru 35.

Core Subject:

Critical thinking and its application within a real world situational context; it is established upon the overarching concept called the Hyper-meta Cognition[SM®] Theoretical Learning Model.

Structural Layout of Assessment:

The test assessment is sub-divided into three core sub-sections—

1. True or False questions (5);
2. Multiple Choice questions (10);
3. Essays questions (2).

Disclaimer Notice: the number within the parenthesis identifies the exact number of items comprised within that distinct assessment-section.

Section One—True or False [Unit 1 & Unit 2]

The following questions are to be answered based upon current understanding of 20 what is true or false. The only requirement circle the most correct or singular response. Notice, the correct answer is found within the parenthesis.

1. One of the chief result of learning critical thinking and the effective application thereof is because it is a productive and positive activity (Brookfield, 1987, p. 5)? (True)
2. The comprehensive learning of critical thinking can result in a greater or higher level of both imagining and the exploration of alternatives (Brookfield, 1987, p. 8)? (True)
3. Learning critical thinking essentially makes one a less competent professional (Brookfield, 1987, p. 12)? (False)
4. One of the greatest benefits of learning critical thinking is that it will ultimately result in my becoming a more successful individual—personally and professionally 30 (Brookfield, 1987, p. 43). (True)
5. Does each individual have the innate ability to tap into and fully develop critical thinking skills (The Jossey-Bass Reader, 2007, p. 7)? (True)

Section Two—Multiple Choice [Unit 2]:

Each underlined section corresponds to an answer choice. The first underlined section corresponds to choice 'A. Kindly select the answer choice that is considered the most accurate answer:

1. Which of the following is a motivation for learning critical thinking (Brookfield, 1995, p. 28)?
     A. I Have Nothing Else to Do
     B. I Am Disinterested in Business Administration
     C. Arriving at a Place of Awareness is a Puzzling Task
     D. To Have a Certificate To Hang Upon the Wall

2. How will taking critical thinking improve my relationship with my colleagues and peers (Brookfield, 1995, p. 28)?
     A. Attempting to Understand My Colleagues-Peers is otherwise a Daunting Task
     B. I Will Become Better Equipped in Manipulating Others
     C. I Will Have the Upper Hand in Applying for a Promotion
     D. It Will Teach Me to Become Telepathic

3. How does learning and mastering critical thinking improve my ability to teach (Brookfield, 1995, p. 39)?
     A. I Have Another Credential to Add To My Resume'
     B. I am Better Apt in Naming & Confronting Dilemmas Plus Contradiction
     C. More People Will Be Impressed By My Abilities
     D. I Am Now More Competitive For Attaining Higher Paying Promotions

4. Critical reflection is a matter of which of the following (Brookfield, 1995, p. 42)?
     A. Stance and Dance
     B. Flight or Fight

    C. Shuck and Jive

    D. Ask and Inquire

5. What does it mean to speak authentically (Brookfield, 1995, p. 45)?

    A. Have a Voice of Persuasion

    B. To Become a More Effective Communicator

    C. To Say What I Mean and Mean What I Say

    D. Alert to the Voices within That Are Not Our Own

6. Which of the following is an important facet of helping people to think critically 10 (Brookfield, 1987, p. 78)?

    A. To Become Vice President of their Organization

    B. To Be Undefeated at Playing Chess

    C. Provide Them an Opportunity to Undertake Periods of Reflective Evaluations

    D. To Learn How to Paint Like Rembrandt

7. According to Gamson & Associates, the Process of Engaging Students for Critical Awareness is best defined as (Brookfield, 1987, p. 80):

    A. Liberating Education

    B. Ought to Be a Degree Program Offered at the University

    C. An Extracurricular Activity

    D. A Process That is Ongoing and Never-ending

8. In reference to the Stages of Development of critical thinking, which of the following is identified as the fourth stage (Paul & Elder, 2006, p. 26)?

    A. Master Thinker

    B. Apathetic Thinker

    C. Hyperactive Thinker

    D. Practicing Thinker

9. Which of the following statements best understood as a summation of critical thinking (Paul & Elder, 2006, p. xvii)?
    A. A Computer Component
    B. Art of Thinking about Thinking
    C. A Pharmaceutical Drug
    D. A Meditative Posture

10. Good thinking requires which of the following (Paul & Elder, 2006, p. xx)?
    A. Hard Work
    B. Vitamin B-12
    C. Unwavering Commitment
    D. A Great Pair of Running Shoes

Section Three—Essay Questions [Unit 1 & Unit 2]:

Students are required to answer the following questions as directly and concise as 15 possible. In fact, the answers should directly correlate with identified or recognized common knowledge within the academic discipline or field of critical thinking.

1. Since enrolling in this course, how have you become more effective in resolving issues on your job?
2. Have you experienced greater positive feedback from your colleagues and peers 20 concerning your ability or relate to and understand others?

Appendix 'B'

Scores:

Section 1—APA Format-Styles (60 possible points)
Section 2—Organization of Ideas and Thoughts (40 possible points) 5

Section 3—Breadth and Depth of Ideas and Insights (50 possible points)

Section 4—Ability to identify, articulate relevance to real world context (70 possible points)

Section 5—Stability of foundation via mechanical and sentence structure (50 possible points)

Section 6—Multiple Choice Questions (35 possible points)

Section 7—True/False Questions (20 possible points)

Total possible points to accrue@ (325 points)

Points and Letter Grade Correlation Scale:

Notice-Instead of listing or categorizing as "collective tabulated points", the grading scale is instead identified in percentile-form. For example, an A+ would range—hypothetically speaking—between 1200 (100%; minimum) points to 1176 (98%; maximum) points; the total points which can be accrued over the length of the residency tabulates at 1200 total points.

[Supplemental Article-Concepts]

Attraction: The Secret of Teaching, Learning, and Leadership

Focus of the Research or Hypothesis:

The focus of the research is the relevancy of "attraction to educational leadership" (Woelfel, 2008, p. 1).

Research Approach Used By the Researcher:

The "Trait Theory Leadership Concept" is used by the author. Peter G. Northouse asserts that great leaders possess "innate qualities and characteristics" (2007, p. 15).

Researcher Conclusions:

Professor Woelfel concludes that attraction is—the secret of effective teaching, learning, and leadership; it is the key attribute that distinguishes the masters from lesser mortals (2008, p. 1).

Description of the Relationship of Research to the Assigned Leadership Theory:

In brief, both the approach utilized by Ms. Woelfel and the assigned leadership theory acknowledges the fact that "effective leaders" possess certain distinguishing attributes.

A Follower's View of Leadership

Focus of the Research or Hypothesis:

The focus of the research is assessing leadership from a "follower's perspective". The author states that a follower can often lose their "correct perspective" (DeSimone, Jr., 2007, p. 1). The article, in brief, thus attempts to assist disillusioned followers in regaining a right perspective.

Research Approach Used By the Researcher:

The "Contingency Approach" to leadership is utilized by the author. It defines "effective leaders" by recognizable attributes, applicable to situational circumstances. Peter G. Northouse affirms that, "a leader's effectiveness depends on how well the leader's style fits the context" (2007, p. 113).

Researcher Conclusions:

In summary, the author insists that effective leadership is comprised of identifiable dimensions, which fluctuates according to situations (DeSimone, Jr., 2007, p. 8). The two key dimensions include the existence for positive change, as well as a desire to endure progressive learning.

Description of the Relationship of Research to the Assigned Leadership Theory:

Consequently, both the author's approach and the assigned leadership theory discuss leadership application according to situational circumstances.

Not on My Watch

Focus of the Research or Hypothesis:

The focus of the research is the balancing act between ensuring cultural diversity and maintaining high quality education; administrators are challenged in ensuring minority students access to programs, as well as maintaining high quality education for all (Evans, 2008, p. 1).

Research Approach Used By the Researcher:

The "Situational Approach" to leadership is used by the author. It is a modality which focuses upon leadership actions contingent upon "situational factors" (Northouse, 2007, p. 113).

Researcher Conclusions:

In summary, Ms. Evans is uncertain as to which side of the collective argument is correct; the "verdict is still out" (2008, p. 3).

Description of the Relationship of Research to the Assigned Leadership Theory:

Consequently, both the research and the assigned leadership theory suffice it addresses critical situational factors, all of which directly affects leadership actions.

QUADRANT II

FIELD OF THE INNOVATIVE MODALITY

The present invention relates generally to a method, apparatus and system. More specifically, the present invention is a new method and system for higher education.

BACKGROUND OF THE INNOVATIVE MODALITY

Transformational Leadership Practices of Teacher Leaders (#4)
Focus of the Research or Hypothesis:

The chief focus of the research is the objective evaluation into the efficaciousness of transformational techniques, as employed by teacher leaders. The objective is achieved by endeavoring into an in-depth and inductive investigative process. Professor Alger avers, "The most significant challenge of leadership is to build and sustain an organizational culture that focuses on continual improvement of educational programs, teachers' capacities and skills, and student learning" (2008, p. 1). In other words, the main issue considers whether teacher leaders are equipped in confronting and thus resolving the vast hindrances, typically faced in an academic environment. The contrasting sides of the argument accordingly are those "whom affirm and believe that teacher leaders can eradicate the recognized barriers", and those that "advocates for the dispersal of leadership authority within a school" (Alger, 2008, p. 1).

Research Approach Used By the Researcher:

The research focal point is achieved by the utilization of a "random sampling" process. The process involves the distribution of invitations, as well as an online survey. The relevant survey is thus comprised of an "LPI and the demographic data form" (2008, p. 2). The "Leadership Practices Inventory"—hence LPI, is sub-divided into two vital components: the "LPI-Self form for teachers and the LPI-Observer form for principals-administrators" (2008, p. 2). This approach demonstrates, in summary, that administrators are well-equipped in addressing-reconciling the sundry of challenges which otherwise might hinder the ultimate objective from becoming realized.

Researcher Conclusions:

Gary Alger thus concludes that the status quo was threatened by the teacher leaders. The author concedes, "The relative strength of teacher leaders was challenging the status quo" (Alger, 2008, p. 4). The teacher leaders in addition were successful in improving the overall quality of life, as well as making significant strides towards achieving the objective. Professor Alger continues "the principals rated the teachers in the top quartile" of the empirical study (p. 4). The teachers on the contrary rated themselves within the mid-quartile range. The results demonstrate that there exists a considerable variance between the peripheral view of administrators and the internal view of teacher leaders.

Professor Alger also exhorts, "principals should become more intimately aware of the work of teacher leaders and the barriers they may be experiencing" (2008, p. 4). Regarding future studies, the author recommends "Principals may wish to consider special support and encouragement for experienced teachers" (2008, p. 4). In summary, teacher leaders might find it challenging in applying transformational strategies and henceforth effectuate lasting progressive change.

Description of the Relationship of Research to the Assigned Leadership Theory:

There exist congruencies between Gary Alger's approach, as well as the "Trait Approach" to leadership. Peter G. Northouse states that great leaders possess "innate qualities and characteristics" (2007, p. 15). The "continual improvement of educational programs, teachers' capacities and skills, and student learning" in any event cannot be achieved, without the application of transformational strategies (Alger, 2008, p. 15). In brief, transformational leaders possess the necessary capacity for formulating both innovation and change, within the context of the academic environment. The objective is hence accomplished by "introducing new beliefs and goals, as well as changing how group members define their responsibilities or roles" (p. 3).

Leading in the Mathematics Classroom (#5)
Focus of the Research or Hypothesis:

The fundamental focus of the research is the objective evaluation of the application of leadership techniques into the classroom environment, yet from a mathematical context. The study is a result of the alarming news concerning the decline in student enrollment, in the fields of "mathematics, science and engineering" (Warick, 2008, p. 1). Jon Warick corroborates that "there has been a sustained year-on-year fall in the numbers of students opting to study mathematics, science, and engineering subjects at degree level" (2008, p. 1). In addition, the interest in mathematics and sciences has arisen because of dual reports received by the United Kingdom Governmental Commission, regarding the "ongoing debate over the quantitative and literacy skills exhibited by students on entry to university courses" (Warick, 2008, p. 1). In brief, the chief objective of the research is to entreat administrators to increase and hence apply leadership techniques, relevant to fields such as mathematics. It is a field nonetheless that has often been "plagued by fear and anxiety, amongst students" (p. 4).

Research Approach Used By the Researcher:

The research focal point is achieved by the utilization of an extensive extrapolative research process. This process is comprised of training modules, leadership models, and "hands-on" experiential learning modalities. In regards to "training modules", they are typically given to first year students. Professor Warick asserts, "My own teaching predominantly involves modules taught to first year students studying for a degree in computing or business information technology" (2008, p. 1). In addition, the students which comprise the target segment include "those from outside the UK, as well as many mature students" (p. 1). In regards to the "leadership models", they include the "classic Kolb Model of experiential learning, and the Hersey and Blanchard Models of Leadership "(2008, p. 1). In brief, leadership is afforded critical tools for the consideration, application, and final revision of current modalities.

Researcher Conclusions:

Jon Warick concludes that a travesty is occurring within the rank-and-file of the global academic community. In other words, rather than fusing the leadership discipline into the systemic process, the opportunity is dissipating. Professor Warick avers "materials are available for developing teacher's management and administrative skills in relation to their teaching but rarely is leadership mentioned" (2008, p. 4). The results are in moreover and it is apparent that leadership is devalued and underutilized. Jon Warick submits a final petition towards administration, that they would consider appropriating the relevant leadership skills at all levels, particularly the faculty. The author submits, "I would like to enter a plea for leadership skills to be discussed at all levels within a teaching institution and in particular for teachers" (2008, p. 4). In brief, it is a crisis in which if not addressed will only become more catastrophic.

Description of the Relationship of Research to the Assigned Leadership Theory:

The existing congruencies between Jon Warick's approach, as well as the "Contingency Theory" of leadership accordingly are as follows. Peter G. Northouse, for starters, affirms that the contingency theory is in fact a "leader-match" theory (2007, p. 113). In other words, the effective application of leadership strategies is contingent upon relevant circumstances. Thus, the efficaciousness of both the contingency theory and Warick's approach depends on the congruency between the leader's style and the circumstantial context. In regards to Warick's approach, lastly, the effective application of leadership techniques is contingent upon the following factors: the leader, the ramifications of cultural diversity, the leader traits in correlation to the followers, and lastly, the quality of relationship between the leader and his followers.

Institutional Servant Leadership (#6)
Focus of the Research or Hypothesis:

The fundamental focus of Brian C. Grizzell's research is the deductive assessment of the constructive ramifications of "servant leadership". In other words, readers are afforded an objectively-unbiased insight into the critical link between servant leadership—at the grassroots level, and the longevity of healthy communal life. Brian C. Grizzell affirms "This paper is a critical essay that discusses the influence of servant leadership on urban community sustainability" (2008, p. 1). In addition, it provides objective analyses into what has already been implemented, as well as the eradication of "chronically destructive" behaviors, all within an urban communal context. The practices utilized conclusively occur at both the "individual-level" and the corporate "institutional-level" (p. 1).

Research Approach Used By the Researcher:

The research focus is achieved through the utilization of diverse investigative techniques, including word-of-mouth, reflective journals, articles, and essays; it is also achieved through information gathered from community partnerships. A brief list of communication channel examples include Dr. Ronald Mason's statement regarding the "grassroots benefactor of servant leadership", Robin Kelley's statement regarding the migration of "upward mobile individuals to the suburbs", Greenleaf's statement regarding "servant leadership" in essence being a "shared leadership model", and lastly, Smiley's suggestions "to strengthen the ability of community members to have input on healthy living decisions affecting them, to increase advocacy skill building, and to actively change the community in its well-being" (Grizzell, 2008, pp. 3-4). In summary, the information gathered was achieved by the researcher's proactively engaging into diverse avenues of communication.

Researcher Conclusions:

Brian C. Grizzell thus concludes that the only avenue or "catalyst" for the longevity of a healthy quality of life within the local-urban community is via the application of "Servanthood strategies" within the leadership paradigm. In addition, it is only through the application of a Servanthood attitude-mentality, within the communal context, that sustainability remains inevitable. Professor Grizzell assertively exhorts, "Servant leaders must also provide a fresh outlook based on their past experiences and contribute to society by meeting its demands in an earnest effort. Exhibiting such behavior definitely may have a positive impact on others; thus inspiring them to do more to help others" (2008, p. 1). In regards to the overall positive impact that servant leadership makes upon the community—globally and locally, the author asserts "True enough, leaders are born, however, they can definitely be made; and the same stands for sustainable urban communities" (p. 6). In the final analysis, the only avenue which guarantees a healthy and sturdy community is the education and hence development of balanced "servant leaders".

Description of the Relationship of Research to the Assigned Leadership Theory:

The apparent congruencies between both Brian C. Grizzell's research approach and the identified "Contingency Approach" to leadership accordingly are as follows. For starters, Peter G. Northouse affirms that the effectiveness of great leaders is contingent upon "situational factors-variables" (2007, p. 113). The theory is, furthermore, at the core "a leader-match theory" (p. 113). In brief, overall effectiveness is achieved if there is congruency between the leader's style and the situational context. In other words, the two distinctly relevant research variables are the attitude or style of the servant leader, and the dire need for servant leaders, applicable within the urban community—consequently, the situational context.

BRIEF DESCRIPTION OF DRAWINGS

FIG. 1 is a flowchart of the Holistically Proactive and Comprehensive Effectiveness System (HPCES) used in the present invention.

DETAIL DESCRIPTIONS OF THE INNOVATIVE MODALITY

CURRICULUM DEVELOPMENT PROJECT (CDP):
Introduction

The chief objective for this project is to afford both author and corresponding readers alike the opportunity to assess the evolution of higher education curriculum. It is the first-of-four total phases, all of which are requisites for completion; the final destination being the "Curriculum Development Project". This section endeavors to draft a paper which examines the challenges of changing global trends, as well as the corresponding conditions. The relevant core sections include:

1. Discuss the ways in which curriculum has evolved.
2. Examine the future of education.
3. Examine current global trends.
4. Discuss predictions for the future of education.
5. Assess the effect of globalization on education.

Ways in Which Curriculum Has Evolved—Traditional to Distance Education

Section one of the CDP; it involves discussing diverse ways in which curriculum has evolved over the past few decades. It involves analyzing the overall transitional-continuum. As a matter of fact, "all organizations and institutions are faced with some significant shifts, resulting from the impact of emerging technologies and a global economy" (Kesim & Agaoglu, 2007, p. 1, ¶1). The core phases, pertinent to this overall project assignment, include the progressive evolution from traditional settings to distance education.

Higher education in the 20ᵗʰ Century is primarily of the traditional academic structure. If an adult learner decides to pursue a college degree, the student is limited in having to enroll at a local community college-university. The core curriculum utilizes textbooks, handouts, and assessments, as well as examination material; it is considered of the traditional method. The subject matter is delivered via discussions, as well as lectures administered by the designate faculty member. Lastly, as it relates to the physical locale, it includes: 1. On-site, the college or university-campus; 2. Pre-designated off-site location.

Education in the 21ˢᵗ Century, however; it is characterized by "a series of technological developments." . . . "One of the new technological developments is called Web 2.0" (Kesim & Agaoglu, 2007, p. 2, ¶3). Regarding the underlying purpose of Web 2.0, it "includes community learning and collaborative learning in a social process" (Kesim & Agaoglu, 2007, p. 2, ¶3). Hence, learning is facilitated utilizing a distance education learning-platform. If an adult learner decides to pursue a college-undergraduate degree, all the students needs to do is connect with the intended school, and thus enroll via telephone, internet, or email medium. In short, instead of having to physically travel to the campus-site, the student can receive the corresponding courseroom-related material via mail, and hence matriculate through the course at one's own self-directed pace.

The core curriculum utilizes: 1. Textbooks; 2. Handouts, and; 3. Diverse learning assessments; 4. Test examination material. The material falls within the category of traditional facilitation methods. The subject matter is delivered via lecturers administered by the delegated faculty and/or pre-recorded group discussion segments. As it relates to the physical locale, it might include: 1. Home; 2. Local library; 3. Any other place considered accessible and convenient.

Examination of the Future of Education

Section two of the CDP; it involves assessing the future of higher education. It includes researching and analyzing the overall direction of the higher education. The first place to commence is with assessing "the 'what' of teacher education" (2006, p. 4, ¶1). It involves investing the necessary energy, resources, and time into re-examining the "many ways of configuring the knowledge that teachers may need" (Darling-Hammond, 2006, p. 4, ¶2). Moreover, the future of 21st Century Education, foundationally involves the comprehensive and thorough preparation of teachers whom are competent and equipped in responding to the diverse challenges, demands, and issues of an ever-changing world. The underlying framework comprises, on one hand, the understanding of teaching being first and foremost a profession; it is considered a "vocational calling". The same framework, on the other hand, considers the reality that learning—the latter part of teaching—is in essence a democratic process. Regarding its *fundamental components*, it includes:

1. Knowledge of Learners & their Development in their Social Contexts;
2. Knowledge of Subject Matter & Curriculum Goals;
3. Knowledge of Teaching (Darling-Hammond, 2006, p. 5, Figure 1).

In a nutshell, this novel approach to learning-curriculum is fused together at the point in which the three aforementioned aspects are intersected, with the overarching philosophy called "A Vision of Professional Practice" (Darling-Hammond, 2006, p. 5, Figure 1). Hence, it is a novel and unconventional approach which literally places greater emphasis-priority upon the often overlooked "discussion about what goes on within the black box of the program" . . . "and about how the experiences programs design for candidates cumulatively add up to a set of knowledge, skills, and dispositions that determine what teachers actually do" within the context of the classroom-setting (Darling-Hammond, 2006, p. 4, ¶1); greater emphasis is placed upon the "preparation of teaching", rather than the typical "traditional teaching process".

Assessment Plus Examination of Current Global Trends

Section three of the CDP; it involves the brief examination of current trends within the realm of global education. Henceforth, we live in such a time that the "quest for knowledge about nature helps mankind advance forward" . . . "Educational institutions also complement the creation of new knowledge by making existing knowledge available in an intelligible format" (Irfan, 2001, p. 1, ¶1). At the *national level*, in fact, "there have been many literatures (e.g., OECD 2000) finding positive correlation between economic growth and educational achievement" (Irfan, 2001, p. 1, ¶2). At the *global level*, moreover, "despite the agreement on the notion of education as a driver of individual or social well being, there are variations across nations along the organization of, investment, and outcomes from education" (Irfan, 2001, p. 1, ¶3). In short, one of the major trends involves an increased awareness into the direct correlation between the facilitation of learning and the overall improvement of well-being—culturally, economically, individually, globally, etcetera.

In addition, there also exists the rising interest in initiating a comprehensive reformation movement within the realm of global higher education. This ever-expanding movement for educational reform—at all levels—is established upon the chief premise that there is indeed an urgent necessity for restoring-revitalizing the "soul of teachers". Hence, this urgent demand for comprehensive reform involves "the establishment of a global policy paradigm in education and social welfare can be identified . . . with the activities of certain key supranatural agencies (World Bank, IMF, OECD) (3)" (Ball, 1999, p. 3, ¶2). In fact, the underlying mechanism of policy convergence is "the shift in many countries from an emphasis on social or mixed social and economic purposes for education to a predominant economic emphasis" (Ball, 1999, p. 3, ¶3). In short, this unprecedented shift in policy-making—at the global level—comprises placing greater emphasis upon the equalization and widespread distribution of otherwise vital financial resources.

Lastly, another major and recognizable global trend involves—Article 26.1 of the Universal Declaration of Human Rights (UDHR)—the overarching necessity for "education must and should contribute to the productive life of every society" (Power, 2000, p. 1, ¶3). In other words, if the chief objective of creating a globalized market is to become realized—per Article 2 of the UDHR—it is imperative that "education shall be directed to the full development of the human personality and to the strengthening of respect for human rights and fundamental freedoms" (Power, 2000, p. 2, ¶1). In short, "it shall promote understanding, tolerance, and friendship among all nations, racial and religious groups" (Power, 2000, p. 2, ¶1). Thus, if the impartial distribution of education is not assertively pursued, then the overall objective for increasing equality and de-polarization will never materialize.

Prediction for the Future of Education

Section four involves a brief evaluation of the overall encompassing prediction germane to the future of higher education. In short, it fundamentally involves critical assess into the classroom of the future—21st Century, and even far beyond.

It appears, for starters, that the main characteristic of the *classroom of the future* is that it is comprised of both advanced cutting-edge technology, and cutting-edge theoretical learning frameworks. Hence, as a direct result of being afforded virtually limitless technology, students will be thoroughly equipped with the necessary instruments, resources, and tools all required for "problem-solving, communication, teamwork, self-assessment, change management, and lifelong learning skills" (Woods, Felder, Rugarcia, and Stice, 2000, p. 1). Thus, the eight basic requisite-activities, all essential in the full development of high level, as well as next-dimension critical thinking and analytical skills includes:

1. Identify the skills you wish your students to develop;
2. Use research, not personal intuition, to identify target skills, and share the research with the students.
3. Make explicit the implicit behavior associated with successful application of the skills.

4. Provide extensive practice in the application of the skills, using carefully structured activities, and provide prompt constructive feedback on the students' efforts using evidence-based targets.

5. Encourage monitoring.

6. Encourage reflection.

7. Grade the process, not just the product.

8. Use a standard assessment and feedback form (Woods, Felder, Rugarcia, & Stice, 2000, pp. 2-4).

In brief, as a direct result of utilizing this novel method for the facilitation of higher academics, students will be equipped, and wholly prepared for arriving at the next-dimension of comprehensive critical thinking.

Assessing the Effect of Globalization on Education

Section five involves assessing the effect of widespread globalization upon the collective sphere of higher education. Professors Altbach, Reisberg, and Rumbley (2009) reveal that "Globalization . . . has profoundly influenced higher education" . . . in fact, it fundamentally is defined by "sending students to study abroad, setting up a branch campus overseas, or engaging in some type of inter-institutional partnership" (p. iv, ¶2). This increasing trend is a direct result of the global conference which transpired in 1990—World Conference on Education for All, held in Jomtein—in which it was "recognized that many of the world's poorest countries lacked the financing capacity that would be necessary to ensure more rapid progress towards universal primary education" (Irfan, 2001, p. 10, ¶1). However, one of the greatest shortcomings of increasing globalization is the gross misallocation of vital financial resources. Thus, "UNDP and others have warned that globalisation is increasing the gap between the rich and the poor, between the connected and isolated cultural groups", as well as indigenous sects of people (Power, 2000, p. 2, ¶7). For the sake of affording a pragmatic direct correlation between the rampant surge in globalization, and it's affirmation for the urgent need of higher education being made available, is the resulting tragic increase in the "upsurge in violence, crime, corruption, and even genocide" (Power, 2000, p. 2, ¶7).

In short, even as there has been a rising demand for the razing of distinct socio-cultural barriers, it is also apparent that there is a vital necessity for the mass availability for higher education to vastly diverse and scattered communities of people. Thus, the primary effect of globalization on higher education is the urgent necessity for making available a quality of higher education that is reflective of excellence. In the end, the global community and her corresponding citizens will be greatly benefited.

Conclusion

The encompassing objective for this project is to afford both author and readers alike the opportunity to assess the evolution of education. Section one; it involves addressing and critically analyzing the overall *learning transitional-continuum*. In short, it endeavors to assess and determine how the learning curriculum has progressed and transformed within the past few decades. Section two; it reveals that the future of higher education—21st Century Education and beyond will focus thereon comprehensive and thorough preparation of teachers whom are competent and equipped in responding to the diverse challenges, demands, and issues of an ever-changing world. Section three; it reveals that at the national level, "there have been many literatures (e.g., OECD 2000) finding positive correlation between economic growth and educational achievement" (Irfan, 2001, p. 1, ¶2). At the global level, moreover, "despite the agreement on the notion of education as a driver of individual or social well being, there are variations across nations along the organization of, investment, and outcomes from education" (Irfan, 2001, p. 1, ¶3). Section four; it divulges that the defining characteristic of the future classroom is that it comprises advanced cutting-edge technology, as well as theoretical learning frameworks. The fifth and final section; it addresses the overarching effect of globalization, as it relates to the realm of higher education. Thus, the urgent demand for making available a quality of higher education that is of the highest standard level. In the end, the global community will be greatly benefited.

References

Altbach, P. G., Reisberg, L., & Rumbley, L. E. (2009). Trends in global higher education: Tracking an academic revolution. A Report Prepared for the UNESCO World Conference on Higher Education. Retrieved July 22, 2011, from http://graduateinstitute. ch/webdav/site/developpement/shared/developpement/cours/ E759/Altbach,%20 Reisberg,%20Rumbley%20Tracking%20an%20Academic%20 Revolution,%20 UNESCO%202009.pdf

Ball, S. J. (1999, September 2-5). Global trends in educational reform and the struggle for the soul of the teacher. Center for Public Policy Research, King's College London. Retrieved July 28, 2011, from http://www.leeds.ac.uk/educol/documents/00001212. htm

Dede, C. (1996). Emerging technologies and distributed learning. The American Journal for Distance Education. Retrieved July 20, 2011, from http://citeseerx.ist.psu.edu/viewdoc/ download?doi=10.1.1.137.5405 &rep=rep1&type=pdf

Hammond, L.D. (2006). Constructing 21st-century teacher education. Journal of Teacher Education, 57. Retrieved July 21, 2011, from http://jte.sagepub.com/content/57/3/300. short

Irfan, M. (2001). Global trends on education. (2001). Retrieved July 19, 2011, from http:// mysite.du.edu/~mirfan/edntrend.pdf

Power, C.N. (2000). Global trends in education. International Education Journal 1(3), 152-163. Retrieved July 21, 2011, from http://ehlt.flinders.edu.au/education/iej/articles/ v1n3/power/begin.htm

Woods, D.R., Felder, R.M., Rugarcia, A., & Stice, J.E. (2000). The future of engineering education: III. Developing critical thinking skills. Chem. Engr. Education, 3(2), pp. 108-117. Retrieved July 23, 2011, from http://citeseerx.ist.psu.edu/viewdoc/download ?doi=10.1.1.43.5906&rep=rep1&type=pdf

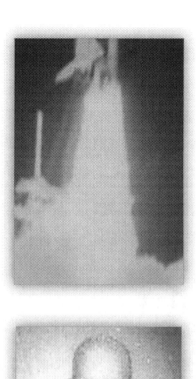

ALA—ASSESSMENT & FRAMEWORKS OF UNDERSTANDING:

Abstract

This application of the Adult Learner Assessment (ALA) Project is to afford both author and target readers alike the opportunity to assess and thus construct a framework through which sound and unwavering understanding both can and will result. It is intended to discuss the overarching learning assessment concept, as well as the drafting and identification of a threshold-line which ultimately distinguishes the fusion point between the theoretical foundation, as well as pragmatic application within a real-world context. The collective project, hence, is sub-divided into four relevant components. These vital ALA components include: 1. Unit 2—Introduction Draft; 2. Unit 5—Assessment Section Draft; 3. Unit 7—Interpretation of Results Draft; 4. Unit 10—Comprehensive Assessment. Pertinent to section one, it is comprised of four core subsections. Pertinent to section two, it is comprised of six core subsections. Pertinent to section three, it is comprised of six core subsections. Pertinent to the fourth and final section, it is comprised of five core subsections. In short, the chief residency-course objective is—at the concluding phase-point—the author will develop a summative assessment, appropriate for the utilization by corresponding adult learners.

Assessment Introduction

The application of the ALA; it is perhaps best understood as an instrument, resource, or tool, that measures the current level of understanding in which students—collectively and individual—have matriculated, all pertinent to the information which was delivered and facilitated. It is a vital utensil which "helps individual college teachers obtain useful feedback on what, how much, and how well their students are learning" (Angelo & Cross, 1993, p. 3). Relevant to its correlation between instruction and the facilitation of assessments, both actually "require that we clearly specify the learning outcomes to be achieved by students, and the provisions of well-designed assessments closely parallel the characteristics of effective instruction" (Gronlund & Waugh, 2009, p. 3). Thus, the most identifiable parallel is, on one hand, the chief purpose is for the utilization of assessment instruments to greatly improve learning facilitation, whereas conversely instruction is merely the facilitation of relevant knowledge which requires the assessment utilization in the first place. Moreover, if maximized and effectively facilitated, the learning assessment will result in improving the overall "effectiveness of many of these decisions by providing more objective information on which to base judgments" (Gronlund & Waugh, 2009, p. 4). Pertinent to the effective completion of unit two—Adult Learner Assessment Introduction, the author addresses and provides relevant substance within the underlying context thereof, as follows: 1. Defining the type and purpose (nature) of the assessment; 2. Identifying and explaining the hypothetical learner subject being covered; 3. Identifying the target learning populations (for example, age, gender, and so on); 4. Identifying at least three learning outcomes to be measured.

Type and Purpose of Assessment

The specific type of assessment being utilized is the Authentic Assessment. Its main purpose is to measure the current level of understanding that the students possess, and how it is relevant to resolving real world challenges and issues. For the sake in fact of being more specific, it concentrates on "real-life tasks (e.g., solving problems that exist in the real world)" (Gronlund & Waugh, 2009, p. 2). In closing, pertinent to the main purpose thereof, it fundamentally "stresses the importance of focusing on the application of understandings and skills to real problems in 'real world'" (Gronlund & Waugh, 2009, p 2) and wholly pragmatic contextual situations. In short, it is an effective way to determine whether the students are equipped and prepared to effectively function and navigate with the set parameters of the real world.

Identify & Explain the Hypothetical Learner—Target Population

The hypothetical learner includes young learners in the age range between eighteen (18) and thirty-five (35). This diverse group of learners falls within the generational groups commonly referred to as: 1. Generation-Y; 2. The Millenials. These same students possess educational experience ranging from right out of high school, junior college, college, graduate, and post-graduate or doctoral-level studies. Hence, it involves the assemblage of diverse students from a broad spectrum of socio-cultural, socio-economic, and socio-religious backgrounds. The economic-status of the student body includes those whom have held part-time level employment-jobs, those whom currently have full-time status, and even entrepreneurs, as well as self-made millionaires. In short, these are best described as a group of students whom are gathered together under an overarching principle called *holistic dynamic (quasi-cultural) participation.*

Identify the Hypothetical Subject

The hypothetical subject is none other than the overarching and ever-dyamic *Critical Thinking Concept.* It is a novel academic discipline which typically falls under the collective field of Professional and Human Development. It is designed, in fact, upon a novel concept—designed and engineered by the author—aptly referred to as The Hyper-meta Cognition^{SM} Theoretical Learning Model (TLM). It is the plane of critical and analytical thinking where the next-dimension of consistently ongoing and unparalleled critical analysis and critical thinking transpires.

Hence, it is established upon the core teaching philosophy that if students are gathered together from vastly diverse and perhaps even convergent parts of the globe, the probability for next-dimension critical thinking is greatly enhanced and increased. As a direct result of providing the necessary information, resources and tools, and thus applying towards challenging and encouraging higher-level critical debate, discussion, and discourse, the student body will matriculate into a distinct class of effective and matured analytical-critical thinkers. It is in short a novel theoretical framework—designed and engineered by the author—aptly named Quantum Acad(yna^{E3})mics^{SM}; it is a critical thinking residency-course that concentrates upon the fusing together of innovation, along with the requisite execution thereof.

Identification of the Core Learning Objectives

Lastly, concerning "**Unit 1—Exactly Why Am I Participating—Underlying Motivations**", the three instructional learning objectives include:

1. Critically assess, examine, and investigate one's underlying motivations—personal and professional.
2. Identify and critically discuss the importance, as well as its relevance to the real-world.
3. Assess the definition of wisdom, and make it applicable to one's individual context.

Concerning "**Unit 2—What is Critical Thinking—Fundamental Intricacies**", the four instructional learning objectives include:

1. Grasp firm understanding of the basics of the brain and cognitive functioning.
2. Understand the direct correlation between mastering one's brain and becoming an effective critical thinker.
3. Be able to skillfully and successfully discuss the quasi-dimensional facets of this subject.
4. Develop a balanced and effective argument. Attempt to persuade others pertinent to one's philosophy & novel viewpoint.

In order for any student to successfully navigate and matriculate through units one and two, he or she must first acquire, and thus master the foundational basics of critical thinking. This learning objective is acutely germane to the first of the three total phases, officially recognized as the *Clay and Pine Phase*.

Conclusion

The application of the Adult Learner Assessment towards the assessment and construction of "Understanding Frameworks" is best understood as an instrument, resource, or tool that measures the current level of understanding in which the body of students have thus matriculated unto.

The chief assessment type being utilized is called the Authentic Assessment. Its main purpose is to address and measure each student's current level of understanding. Also how it is directly relevant to resolving real world challenges, issues, and situations. It is an effective way to determine whether the students are equipped and prepared to function and navigate in the real world.

The hypothetical learner—target population, includes young learners in the age range between eighteen and thirty-five. This diverse group of learner falls within the generational groups commonly referred to as: 1. Generation-Yers; 2. The Millenials.

The hypothetical subject is Critical Thinking. It is a novel academic discipline which falls under the field of Professional and Human Development. It is a novel theoretical framework aptly named The |Quantum| Acad(yna^{E3})mics^{SM} Strategic System. Concerning both units one and two, moreover, in order for any student to successfully matriculate, he or she must first acquire and master the foundational basics of critical thinking.

References

Angelo, T.A. & Cross, K.P. (1993). *Classroom assessment techniques: A handbook for college teachers*. (2nd ed.). San Francisco, CA: Jossey-bass.

Gronlund, N.E., & Waugh, C.K. (2009). *Assessment of student achievement*. (9th ed.). Upper Saddle River, NJ: Pearson-Merrill.

APPLICATION AND IMPORTANCE OF ETHICS:

Abstract

Ethics Reflection both assesses and examines the correlation between the ethical concept and its relevancy within the academic-research context. Each participant has the opportunity to reflect thereon the importance and process of ethics. The information is extrapolated directly from the course readings, ethics and IRB media pieces, and the Office of Research and Scholarship Web site. It thus comprises the following questions: 1. What general characteristics of qualitative and quantitative research methods could propose ethical issues; how would you rectify these situations; 2. Describe three strengths and weaknesses each of qualitative and quantitative research methods as they relate to ethics; 3. Why is it important for a research methodology to support a research question; 4. Why is it important that the data collection methods of a study support the research methodology; 5. What can you do to expedite the IRB process when you are at that stage in your program.

Foundational Premise

A qualitative research method is understood as a practice of interpretive or field research; it utilizes methodologies that have been borrowed from disciplines like sociology and anthropology and adapted to educational settings (Lodico, Spaulding, and Voegtle, 2010, p. 142). It focuses thereon the critical and investigative study of "social phenomena and on giving voice to the feelings and perceptions of the participants under study" (Lodico, Spaulding, and Voegtle, 2010, p. 142).

Conversely, the quantitative research method places greater weight or emphasis upon the acquisition of pertinent and vital statistical data findings. It thus involves the comparison of "the effects of teacher experience, neighborhood socioeconomic level, and age of students on ratings of feeling safe", (Jones and Kottler, 2006, p. 29) as a prime example thereof.

Next, pertinent to the encompassing *concept of ethics*, it is perhaps best understood as the comprehensive, yet systematic concept upon which such fundamental virtues as uprightness of character, uncompromising integrity, and human decency is established thereon. It attempts to set necessary boundaries that essentially preserves and protects a set standard of codes, policies, and procedures from not being compromised-violated; this is because of the deterrence caused by the fear of public criticism, rebuke, scorn, and etcetera. As it correlates to the overall idea of research ethics, it is indeed "an important consideration" (Lodico, Spaulding, and Voegtle, 2010, p. 16).

Also, according to the Belmont Report, the three fundamental ethical principles merely footnote that "researchers must observe as they design and execute their studies includes the respect for persons, beneficence, and justice ("Capella University Research Center", 2011). Hence, it is the responsibility of the researcher to ensure that every participant is first and foremost protected from damage, harm, or injury. Secondly, to ensure that the underlying benefits thereof are fully maximized, with risk held to a minimum; thirdly, also guaranteeing that there is both a fair and impartial distribution between the burdens, as well as the benefits of participating therein. In short, there exists the ongoing endeavor to maintain a system of balance such that the highest level of efficiency, productivity, and success is fully manifested and realized.

Characteristics of Qualitative & Quantitative Research Methods

What general characteristics of qualitative and quantitative research methods could propose ethical issues, and how would you rectify these situations? Please provide specific examples.

The general characteristics of both methods which might cause ethical issues, literally begins and ends with using people as data sources. Thus, if the proper procedures and protocols are not implemented, the comprehensive process itself can result in damage, harm and injury to the corresponding target participant-body. For example, just within "recent years we have become increasingly aware that research using people may inadvertently harm them—not just physically but by embarrassing them, violating their privacy, and so on" (Booth, Colomb, and Williams, 2008, p. 83). As a direct result, practically every institution of higher learning has a select committee—Human Subject Committee, which addresses and responds-resolves such related issues.

In a nutshell, the specific list of qualitative and quantitative-related characteristics include: 1. The information gathered might be inaccurate and grossly filled with errors and flaws; 2. The overall system of vital data acquisition might be considered acutely haphazard. Next, it continues; 3. The confidentiality of the target participants can be violated resulting in vast legal ramifications which will undermine and sabotage the overall organizational success; 4. The context and nature of the research study—qualitative or quantitative, might not pragmatically reflect the encompassing socio-cultural climate and setting for which the study itself was initially intended, to name but a few.

Regarding the *second aspect* of how will the ethically compromising situation be rectified, the answer is in fact three-tiered. The <u>first-tier</u> involves asking the right questions and finding the right answers. In short, the chief objective is to "have a plan and take one step at a time" (Booth, Colomb, and Williams, 2008, p. 31). The <u>second-tier</u> involves wholly ensuring that the initial claim posed is both effectively and sufficiently supported, thus reinforced with sound empirical-factual evidence. In short, it is imperative that every hypothetical-claim is likewise provided with a solution that is firmly sound and unwavering. Hence, the researcher must exhaust every effort in ensuring that the claim is backed up with two rudimentary types of support: reasons and evidence (Booth, Colomb, and Williams, 2008, p. 110). The <u>third-tier</u> involves investing the necessary resources—energy, time, and otherwise, in planning, constructing, and making the requisite revisions as deemed necessary. In short, the researcher needs to ensure that from the onset, a cycle of perpetual analysis, if you prefer, is thoroughly developed. Hence, it essentially involves a comprehensive system of "writing summaries, analyses, and critiques from the start" (Booth, Colomb, and Williams, 2008, p. 173). In the end, this will prevent the misuse of vital resources, as well as the violation of ethical standards that ultimately will sabotage lasting organizational success.

Strengths & Weaknesses Each of Qualitative & Quantitative Research

Describe three strengths and weaknesses each of qualitative and quantitative research methods as they relate to ethics?

The *first strength* of the **qualitative research method** is that it focuses upon vital information that can directly address and thus respond to real world challenges, issues, and situations. It can also be interpreted as a brand of phenomenological research; it is "the study of everyday, lived experiences and the meaning that people construct form them" (Lodico, Spaulding, and Voegtle citing McClelland, 1997, p. 108; 2010, p. 148). On the other hand, the *first weakness* is that is runs the risk of assuming that the pulse of the group selected reflects that of the larger body of society. Thus, there is the possibility that the information is accurate and filled with diverse inaccuracies and inconsistencies. In short, the key determining factor as to whether the method presents itself as a strength or weakness is the overall quality of the gathered information; is it accurate or is there evidence of flaw, this is the operative question.

The *second strength* is that it directly addresses and focuses thereon information germane to the concept and notion of interpersonal relationships. In short, it can be interpreted as a brand of ethnographic research. It's fundamental philosophy and overarching purpose is "to discover the patterns of culture and its unique complexities in order to 'paint a portrait' of the group, its interactions, and its setting" (Lodico, Spaulding, and Voegtle, 2010, p. 151). LeCompte and Schensul (1999) assert that "it is useful in the discovery of knowledge that is embedded within a culture or community" (Lodico, Spaulding, and Voegtle, 2010, p. 151). On the other hand, the *second weakness* is that is runs the risk of taking for granted the underlying diverse challenges and issues germane to human interpersonal relationships. In short, the key determining factor as to whether the method presents itself as a strength or weakness is the overall amount plus quality of energy, resources, and time to thoroughly investigate the target participant-body. Thus, the operative question is; *has substantive resources invested towards a high quality of research thus becoming realized*?

The *third strength* is that it presents data that can be easily interpreted, through the utilization, thus core emphasis placed upon verbal descriptions of the characteristic being investigated. In short, it can also be interpreted as a brand of narrative inquiry; it "assumes that we all lead 'storied lives' and that educators and learners are both 'story tellers and characters in their own and others' stories'" (Lodico, Spaulding, and Voegtle citing Connelly& Clandinin, p. 2; 2010, p. 144). On the other hand, the *third weakness*is that is runs the risk of ignoring and overlooking the quandary of issues that results and thus occurs in a culturally diverse market. In short, the key determining factor as to whether the method presents itself as a strength or weakness is in response to the question of whether or not the foundational language is translated into other languages acutely relevant to the target participant-body. Thus, the operative question is, will the language utilized therein be one that is sufficiently sensitive to the corresponding socio-cultural sect for which it correlates?

The *first strength* of the **quantitative research method**, however, is that it has the potential for providing vital information that is accurate and thus reflects the current socio-cultural pulse. It can also be interpreted as a brand of trend study; it is "typically used to examine the perceptions of groups that are having or have had a shared experience at a particular point in time" (Lodico, Spaulding, and Voegtle, 2010, p. 199). On the other hand, the *first weakness* is that in the process of becoming hyper-consumed with trends, the overall approach utilized thereof becomes one-dimensional and in the long run will result in the loss and otherwise flagrant misuse of vital resources.

The *second strength* is that, divergent to the qualitative method, greater effort is often afforded to the creation and utilization of pragmatic surveys. In short, it can be interpreted as a brand of descriptive critical research, thus utilizing demographic-surveys. Surveys that concentrate thereon socio-cultural demographics are in fact "descriptors that provide detailed information about participants in the study" (Lodico, Spaulding, and Voegtle, 2010, p. 208). This type of quantitative study if often characterized as being concise, specific, and tightly managed. On the other hand, the *second weakness* is that in the attempt to complete the comprehensive survey within a predetermined amount of time, there is the risk that if push comes to shove, corners will be cut and shortcuts will thus be taken.

The *third strength* is that it presents data that can be easily interpreted, through the utilization, thus core emphasis upon verbal descriptions of the characteristic being investigated. In short, it can also be interpreted as a brand of narrative inquiry; it "assumes that we all lead 'storied lives' and that educators and learners are both 'story tellers and characters in their own and others' stories'" (Lodico, Spaulding, and Voegtle citing Connelly& Clandinin, p. 2; 2010, p. 144). Hence, this uniquely personal narrative story is then effectively developed and thus applied in a context applicable to others—key and shadowy contemporaries, thereof. On the other hand, the *third weakness* is that the underlying issues—personal, social, and otherwise, that often undermine the overall integrity of the research process can be ignored or even grossly underestimated; in such that lasting comprehensive success can be hindered and even subverted.

Importance for a Research Methodology to Support

Why is it important for a research methodology to support a research question in terms of ethics?

The main or encompassing reason as to why it is imperative for a research methodology to support a research question is to "ensure that all research conducted under the review of Capella University meets the highest ethical standards and complies with the federal regulations for the protection of human participants in research" (Capella University Research Center citing the overall mission of the Human Research Protection Program (HRPP), 45.CFR.46; 2011)). Thus, it is important for the researchers place greater emphasis upon identifying and implementing a direct linear-correlation between the methodology, as well as the corresponding question utilized and thus facilitated. This will not only preserve and protect the overall research's credulity, but most importantly guarantee that the diverse research intricacies are reliable and resolute. The key characteristics, in fact, of a reliable research are:

1. A study that uses the scientific method, which includes a research hypothesis, a treatment group, and a control group;
2. A study that can be replicated and generalized;
3. A study that meets rigorous standards in design, methods used, and interpretation of the results;
4. A study that produces convergent findings, for example, findings are consistent using various approaches" (Lodico, Spaulding, and Voegtle, 2010, p. 4).

Moreover, the underlying notion supporting correlation prediction studies "examines whether a measure taken at one time can predict a later behavior; researchers must be able to link the two measures taken by each participant" (Lodico, Spaulding, and Voegtle, 2010,

p. 279). This will consequentially guarantee in short that the overall quality of the research meets the highest standards, as well as ensuring that any possible challenges or hindrances, that might otherwise subvert the success of the research be averted and prevented; ethics is both achieved and maintained.

Importance That the Data Collection Methods Support

Why is it important that the data collection methods of a study support the research methodology?

The main or encompassing reason as to why is it important that the data collection methods of a study support the research methodology is to ensure that avoid any risk for the manifestation of error. In other words, by investing the necessary resources in establishing a firm and unwavering foundation, the ultimate objective for engaging in the comprehensive research process from the onset will be achieved. In fact, this approach to active critical research falls there under the category of action research. This brand of critical research endeavors to "improve education" (Lodico, Spaulding, and Voegtle, 2010, p. 328), above all else. Pritchard (2002) asserts that action research often involves sensitive ethical issues and questions; it fundamentally is comprised of two main or entangled goals: improving practice and advancing educational knowledge (Lodico, Spaulding, and Voegtle, 2010, p. 328).

Ultimately, in the long run this will for the most part guarantee that the direct link between both the underlying reasoning premise and the resulting evidence thereof is both consistent and soundly established. After all, if the readers of corresponding participants "think those reasons make consecutive sense, they will look for the evidence they rest on, the bedrock of every argument" (Booth, Colomb, and Williams, 2008, p. 130). Conversely, if the same players do not "believe the evidence, they'll reject the reasons, and with them the claim" (Booth, Colomb, and Williams, 2008, p. 130). Thus, the underling notion concentrates thereon the requisite issue involving the critical and vital need for a foundation that, over the course of test and time, will not falter or fail.

Expediting the IRB Process

Finally, what can you do to expedite the IRB process when you are at that stage in your program?

The most important step is making sure that a firm understanding is acquired, as it pertains to what the IRB is and what is its underlying purpose thereof. In other words, the first objective is in ensuring that it is clearly understood that IRB is an ensemble of "institutional review boards whose members review proposals for research to determine if ethical issues have been considered" (Lodico, Spaulding, and Voegtle, 2010, p. 16).

Next, makes haste in investigating and thus "finding out who will review proposal and the procedures you that will need to be followed in order to thus obtain the inevitable approval status "(Lodico, Spaulding, and Voegtle, 2010, p. 16). Hence, this will eliminate a significant amount of wasteful time in knowing exactly who the key players will be involved in ultimately passing the submitted proposal and thus making the critical decision. It is a decision that will ultimately determine whether it is approved or conversely rejected.

Conclusion

The purpose for the Ethics Reflection is to assess and examine the identifiable correlation between the ethical concept and its relevancy within an academic research context. Pertinent to the general characteristics of the qualitative and quantitative research methods, it begins and ends at the point when people are utilized as data sources. In regards to the second aspect addressing how the ethically compromising situation will be rectified, the answer is in fact three-tiered.

Next, regarding the three strengths and weaknesses of the quantitative research method, the key determining factor as to whether the method presents itself as a strength or weakness is whether or not the foundational language is translated into other languages relevant to the target body of participants. Regarding the three strengths and weaknesses of the qualitative research method, the key determining factor involves whether or not the resulting elements of the overall narrative process is indeed accurate and without flaw.

Moreover, pertinent towards ensuring that the research methodology supports a research question in term of ethics, the answer is that it guarantees that the overall research quality meets the highest standards. It also ensures that all possible challenges-hindrances, that might otherwise subvert the research's success is ultimately averted and prevented.

Regarding the question why is it important that the data collection methods of a study support the research methodology; the direct response is concentrates thereon vital need for a foundation that, over the course of test and time, will not ultimately falter.

Lastly, in response to the issue; what can you do to expedite the IRB process when you are at that stage in your program, the answer is succinctly that the most important step is suffice in ensuring that a that a firm understanding is acquired. In short, the two core questions which are addressed includes: 1. what is the IRB; 2. what is its underlying purpose thereof.

References

Booth, Colomb, & Williams. (2008). *The craft of research*. (3rd ed.). Chicago, IL: The University of Chicago Press.

Capella University Research Center. (2011). Ethical Principles. Retrieved April 28, 2011, from http://www.capella.edu/researchCenter/ethicalPrinciples.aspx

Capella University Research Center. (2011). Human Research Protection Program (HRPP). Retrieved April 28, 2011, from http://www.capella.edu/researchCenter/HRPP.aspx

Jones & Kottler. (2006). *Understanding research: Becoming a competent and critical consumer*. Upper Saddle River, NJ: Pearson-Merrill Prentice Hall.

Lodico, Spaulding, & Voegtle. (2010). *Methods in educational research: From theory to practice*. (2nd ed.). San Francisco, CA: Jossey-Bass.

ANALYSIS OF QUALITATIVE DATE:

Abstract

The process of analyzing *Qualitative Data*; it affords the researcher-author and readers the opportunity to engage therein the data analysis process. It involves the analysis of the interview complexities applicable to the qualitative research methodology. Once the interview has been completed and transcribed, the six steps of qualitative data analysis is then applied.

The six steps of qualitative data analysis includes: (a) Preparation and data organization; (b) Data review and exploration; (c) Categorization of coded data; (d) Construction of diverse thick descriptions; (e) Theme building and hypotheses testing; (f) Data reporting and germane interpretation. Applicable to the six step infrastructure, it includes a brief reflective statement of the core process utilized. The reflection is comprised of the following aspects: (a) what was experienced; (b) what was learned; (c) what is considered difficult, easy, interesting, or etcetera. Lastly, the assignment includes the encompassing chief research question, as well as both the introduction and concluding paragraphs.

Fundamentals of Qualitative Research

The Qualitative Research Method (QRM) is a practice of interpretive research. QRM facilitates methodologies borrowed from academic disciplines like sociology and anthropology; it is adapted to educational settings (Lodico, Spaulding, & Voegtle, 2010, p. 142). This method concentrates thereon the critically investigative study of "social phenomena and on giving voice to the feelings and perceptions of the participants under study" (Lodico, Spaulding, & Voegtle, 2010, p. 142). The method endeavors to assess those items considered as relevant to the underlying study focus. Acquired information is considered reflective of the main pulse-voice, pertinent to the core objectives of the interview study. The method is best summarized with stating that researcher's support their underlying claim with information that has not been fully collected, let alone processed. Qualitative researchers "review their data as they are collected and record and write up their hunches, initial analyses, and questions in the form of research memos" (Lodico, Spaulding, & Voegtle, 2010, p. 180). The qualitative research method is characterized as an inductive process. The three main strengths of qualitative research includes: (a) focuses upon vital information that addresses and responds to real world challenges, issues, and situations; (b) focuses thereon information relevant to the concept and notion of interpersonal relationships; (c) presents data that can be easily interpreted, through the utilization and core emphasis being placed upon verbal descriptions of the characteristic being investigated. The overall quality of the information is considered relevant to the real-world, core essence of interpersonal relationships, and data that is simple enough for full interpretation.

Introduction of Research

The chief purpose for the overall scientific research process is investigating information considered acutely germane to the study—at the individual and/or organizational-level. It is understood as "studying in order to acquire information or applying one's mind to the acquisition of knowledge" (Jones & Kottler, 2006, p. 5). A significant portion of the information is considered as the defining factor which results in the quality of the study being considered as successful or otherwise a total failure. Even as in the case for example of the theme of this assignment, the results answer the core research question, Does engaging therein critical thinking improve one's ability for effectively fusing together innovation along with pragmatic, hence effective execution thereof?

Marzano, Walters, & McNulty (2003) reveals that "students in effective schools as opposed to ineffective schools have a 44 percent difference in the expected passing rate on a test that has a typical passing rate of 50 percent" (2005, p. 3). The core factor which ultimately distinguishes School 'A' from School 'B', as it pertains to the notion of effectiveness, is whether or not the student body has mastered the critical thinking fundamentals. The encompassing purpose for qualitative research is to "Let us have faith that right makes right; and in that faith let us to the end dare to do our duty as we understand it" (Lincoln, 1998, p. 276). The author's essential theory in action is that research involves nothing more and nothing less than engaging in the ongoing and never-ending quest for clear and unbridled understanding. Argyris and Schön (1974) asserts that a theory in action "is a theory of deliberate human behavior, which is for the agent a theory of control but which, when attributed to the agent, also serves to explain or predict his behavior" (p. 6). The research endeavors to acquire information which in the end provides understanding.

Research Question

Does engaging therein critical thinking improve one's ability for effectively fusing together innovation along with pragmatic, hence effective execution thereof?

The ultimate objective for developing high-level critical thinking skills is the matriculation of students whom are effective, skilled, and competent critical thinkers; it is referred to by the author as *Masters of Hyper-meta Cognition*[SM]. Individuals who arrive at this dimension of critical thinking not only possess a greater understanding of what it takes to bridge the gap between innovation and execution, but more importantly, being able to apply this same knowledge within the context of their dynamic spheres of influence. They will have the tools and resources for assisting others in becoming effective systematic facilitators of critical thinking. These individuals will become passionate philanthropic coaches, mentors, professionals, and teachers, existing again within their corresponding scopes and diverse realms of influence. If critical thinking is lacking even one iota, as it applies to the fusion interaction formula—innovation's direct interaction with execution, success will more than likely become realized. Critical thinking exists as the fundamental driving force which positions the student for not only identifying the essential sub-components of innovation, but also effectively discern the most correct timing for implementing what has already been decided, all germane to the specific system for which it is acutely intended. Browne and Keeley (1998) admonishes that "Before we evaluate someone's reasoning, we must first find it" (p. 13). If one has never endeavored to develop and train their otherwise undeveloped or underdeveloped critical thinking muscles, hence abilities, he or she will be ultimately be ill-equipped in identifying the pertinent core issues and thus arrive at a most desirable conclusion.

Prepare and Organize the Data

The main objective for preparing and organizing the data is to lay a concrete—sound and unwavering foundation upon which the overall Qualitative Data Analysis rests thereon. It serves to "make sure that data are in a form that can be easily analyzed" (Lodico, Spaulding, & Voegtle, 2010, p. 180). This preparation and organization process essentially saves energy, resources, and time as it pertains to cutting through distractions, as well as diverse forces which can ultimately hinder the overall research itself. In fact, Lodico, Spaulding, & Voegtle (2010) reveals that "most qualitative researchers prefer to separate the process of data preparation and analysis by transcribing interviews verbatim" (p. 181). Pertinent to the interview, the gathered information is transcribed and document exactly in the form and fashion in which it the dialogue was exchanged; the gathered data is copied and recorded verbatim. The main objective for diligently focusing thereon comprehensive and thorough systematic organization is to greatly improve the overall quality of the comprehensive research process.

Pertinent to the interview, the next step which occurs is the categorization of the data according to distinct attributes-classes. The five common methods of structural organization embedded within the preparation and organization process: (a) Site or location from which data were collected; (b) Person(s) or group studied; (c) Chronological order; (d) Type of data; (e) Type of event of issue addressed (Lodico, Spaulding, & Voegtle, 2010, p. 182). Pertinent to the corresponding process actively engaged, it commences with defining and approaching critical thinking as a systematic concept and endeavor. Critical thinking is understood as "recognizing the assumptions underlying our beliefs and behaviors. It means we can give justifications for our ideas and actions" (Brookfield, 1987, p. 13). The comprehensive process involves students attempting to rationalize and thus acquire understanding, all pertinent to their scopes and spheres of influence. The comprehensive process involves thinking and reasoning within the context of a reflective dimension. As it pertains to that which is considered as either difficulty, easy, interesting, or etcetera, the author-interviewer finds it most intriguing, as well as interesting that critical thinking is a fundamental part of everyday functioning and living—personal and professional relevance.

Review and Explore the Data

The main objective for data review and exploration is to invest the necessary resources, essential in critically assessing and interpreting the data. During this step, gathered data are essentially divided into distinct categories. Pertinent to the first category, it is entitled Underlying Motivational Factors. The second category is likewise entitled as Benefits of Critical Thinking in a Real-world Context. The third category is entitled as Information Directly Corresponding to Previous Experiences. Nevertheless, the main reason for engaging there such a futile process is because "a qualitative researcher might look with dread at the enormous pile of data waiting for analysis" (Lodico, Spaulding, & Voegtle, 2010, p. 182). Thus, the direct result thereof is for the sake of making the overall research study efficient. Moreover, the underlying purpose for getting involved and remaining committed is to "immerse oneself in the data and gain a sense of its possibilities" (Lodico, Spaulding, & Voegtle, 2010, p. 182).

Pertinent to the corresponding process actively engaged, it commences with acquiring a firm grasp of the process for gaining understanding. Checking for understanding is "an important step in the teaching and learning process" (Fisher & Frey, 2007, p. 2). The acquisition of understanding endeavors to ultimately assess the end result. Pertinent to the interview, the gathered date is considered essential for the overall study being considered most successful. Checking for understanding provides students with a model of good study skills; "when their teachers regularly check for understanding, students become increasingly aware of how to monitor their own students" (Fisher & Frey, 2007, p. 3). The main advantage for gaining understanding is to guarantee that the encompassing quality of the research process is well worth the energy and time.

Coding Data into Distinctive Categories

The main objective for the categorization of coded data is the identification of diverse sub-components and thus the drafting of a direct correlation between each distinct segment. The overall activity of data coding is "the process of identifying different segments of the data that describe related phenomena and labeling these parts using broad category names" (Lodico, Spaulding, & Voegtle, 2010, p. 183). Once the process has been completed, and the researcher is at ease with the results, "the next step is to use the codes to organize data and construct descriptions of the data" (Lodico, Spaulding, & Voegtle, 2010, p. 184). The next step of formally drafting and thus constructing the defining attributes which distinguishes the corresponding people, places, and event factors one from the other, is thus commenced.

Pertinent to the corresponding process engaged, it commences with acquiring a firm grasp of the process necessary for gaining understanding. Hence, checking for understanding is "an important step in the teaching and learning process" (Fisher & Frey, 2007, p. 2). The main purpose for the acquisition of understanding is to assess the end result thereof. The checking for understanding provides students with a model of good study skills. That is "when their teachers regularly check for understanding, students become increasingly aware of how to monitor their own students" (Fisher & Frey, 2007, p. 3). The main advantage for gaining balanced understanding is to guarantee that the underlying and encompassing quality of the research process is well worth the resources—energy and time.

TABLE 1.1 Code Data into Distinct Categories

Code Category	Code Names
Interview purpose	Gather data, assess-process data, facilitate data
Time constraints	Five minutes, ten minutes, fifteen minutes
Context and quality of data	Concise and succinct; vague and general
Underlying interview provocation	Personal appreciation; considered relevant
Previous experience with subject	Expansive, limited, none
Critical thinking defined Discovery	Way of knowing, thinking, understanding; Idea
How critical thinking will be utilized data	Learn novel information; Reciprocate current

Construct Thick Descriptions of People, Places, and Activities

The main objective for the construction of thick descriptions of people, places, and activities, is to fundamentally identify the core and underlying descriptions, hence underlying attributes of the corresponding people, places, and event factors thereof. In other words, it essentially includes the establishment and construction of main categories under which the diverse and uniquely distinct people, places, and activity factors can thus be categorized therein.

Thus, the main objective is to "provide rich, in-depth descriptions of the experiences, perspectives, and physical settings represented in the data" (Lodico, Spaulding, & Voegtle, 2010, p. 185). In a nutshell, it literally involves the active researcher or student "expanding on one's field notes and combining notes and interviews with the same codes into more integrated descriptions of people, situations, and places" (Lodico, Spaulding, & Voegtle, 2010, p. 185). Hence, the encompassing concept is the construction of core, yet vitally imperative categories.

Pertinent to the corresponding process actively engaged, it fundamentally involves the assembling and erecting of a matrix for reasoning of the gathered and organized data findings or empirical evidence thereof. Booth, Colomb, & Williams (2008) affirm that "when you order your reasons, you outline the logical structure of your argument. You can do that in a traditional outline, but you may find it more useful to create a chartlike outline" (p. 130). In other words, the ultimate benefit for organizing and structuring the data findings into distinct and separate categories is for the sake of laying a firm and unwavering foundation. It is necessary for the overall success of the comprehensive research activity becoming realized. In short, once this phase—construction of pertinent attributes and descriptions, is officially accomplished, the next step of erecting an encompassing theme, as well as the testing of the underlying hypotheses can thus commence.

Build Themes and Test Hypotheses

The main objective for the building of themes and the testing of the hypotheses, is for the constructing of a firm and sturdy foundational framework, upon which the diverse organizational ideas will be erected and thus remain thereon. In fact, the theme is nothing more than the vast ideas that link or "combine several codes in a way that allow the researcher to examine the qualitative subquestions guiding the research" (Lodico, Spaulding, & Voegtle, 2010, p. 185). Hence, they are typically referred to "in a few words or phrases, but they identify the major concepts or issues that the researcher uses to interpret and explain the data" (Lodico, Spaulding, & Voegtle, 2010, p. 185).

Next, regarding the hypotheses, it exists as the temporal or intermediate presumptions which essentially explain the formal "processes underlying what has been observed" (Lodico, Spaulding, & Voegtle, 2010, p. 189). In short, it is summarized as the core explanation which has been drafted and formulated, all for the sake of affording at the very least initial evidence for active consideration.

Pertinent to the interview, in closing, the underlying, yet encompassing theme is that critical thinking is a vital and relevant part of everyday living. It is so imperative, in fact, that the lack of becoming engaged can ultimately affect and undermine the success of leaders—current and future-context. Next, the interviewee considers critical thinking as a major part of his overall success in life. The interviewer also considered it a responsibility of his to actively participate therein this overall study. Pertinent to his working experience with critical thinking, it goes all the way back to his earliest developmental years. Pertinent to the interviewee definition and interpretation of critical thinking, it is considered as the underlying way of knowing, thinking, and understanding; it is considered as a natural trait intrinsic within all individuals. Lastly, pertinent to how the interviewee foresees critical thinking being a major part of his future career, it will afford a priceless opportunity to learn and acquire novel information. Also, this self-mastery in the long run will be fully reciprocated back to the collective "Critical Thinking Academia". Hence, it is considered vital towards the facilitation of high-level critical thinking within the context of the *Economics of 360-degree Critical Thinking*, aka "Reflective Academics Matriculation".

Report and Interpret Data

The main objective for the reporting and interpretation of pertinent data is the organization of the data findings which has been acquired throughout the totality of the research process. This process is defined as the formal "researcher's interpretation of what the data means" (Lodico, Spaulding, & Voegtle, 2010, p. 192). Pertinent to the overall context of the processed research data findings, it is for the most part, processed and structurally organized in a "nonquantitative, narrative manner, which often makes it enjoyable to read" (Lodico, Spaulding, & Voegtle, 2010, p. 192). Only after the information has been formally processed, and facilitated in a report form, the next step involves interpreting qualitative data by "making sense of the 'lessons learned' by looking for their larger meaning. Interpretation might involve relating the findings to previous published studies or to a theoretical framework" (Lodico, Spaulding, & Voegtle, 2010, p. 193). It comprises the necessary data findings considered germane to the successful completion of the comprehensive research study. The main idea is to rightly interpret and thus effectively facilitate the pertinent gathered data findings.

Conclusion

The overall purpose for this Qualitative Research Method is to afford understanding pertinent to the encompassing practice of interpretive-field research. Hence, there is the assessment of information considered germane and vital towards the encompassing study. Pertinent to the overall objective, it concentrates thereon the correlation of high-level critical thinking skills applicable to the matriculation of students whom are effective, skilled, and competent individuals.

Regarding the first step—**preparing and organizing the data**; it involves laying a sound and unwavering foundation upon which the overall Qualitative Data Analysis rests. It involves data exploration, investing the necessary resources, as well as critically reviewing the interview data which ultimately is applicable to the comprehensive research process. The author's direct reaction is that this is indeed the most fundamental of all six steps. Thus, without investing substantive time in preparing and organizing the data, all other attempts to successfully navigate throughout the entire process will inevitably fail. In direct response to what changes would be made if the interview was to be conducted again; the answer is to include at the least a total of ten relevant questions.

Regarding the second step—**reviewing and exploring the data**; it involves investing the necessary resources in assessing and reviewing the data applicable to the comprehensive research process. This is the step in which the comprehensive data is classified into three fundamental categories. Pertinent to the interview, the gathered information is considered essential for the overall study being considered most successful. The author's response is that engaging therein the reviewing and exploring of data is vitally important for effectively separating data considered relevant from data considered irrelevant. In direct response to what changes would be made if the interview was to be conducted again; the answer is nothing at all.

Regarding the third step—**coding data into distinct categories**; it involves the assessment and identification of diverse sub-components, as well as the drafting of a direct correlation between each distinct segment. While engaged therein this step, the comprehensive data that is gathered is classified into three fundamental and relevant categories. Pertinent to the interview, the identified classifications includes: (a) Interview purpose; (b) Time constraints; (c) Context and quality of data; (d) Underlying interview provocation; (e) Previous experience with subject; (f) Critical thinking defined; (g) How critical thinking will be utilized. In direct response to what changes would be made if the interview was to be conducted again; the answer is nothing at all; the overall classifications are considered effective.

Regarding the fourth step—**constructing think descriptions**; it involves the identification of the core, yet underlying descriptions, applicable to the corresponding people, places, and event factors thereof. Hence, the main objective is the building of themes and testing the hypotheses, it is for the sake of constructing an unwavering foundational framework, upon which the diverse organizational ideas will be erected and thus remain. In direct response to what changes would be made if the interview was to be conducted again; the answer is nothing at all; the overall classifications are considered effective.

Regarding the fifth step—**building themes and testing hypotheses**; it involves the construction of a firm foundation. During this step, the identifiable codes are constructed and linked up in such a way that the underlying core objective or hypotheses for the assignment is identified; the chief hypotheses is that engaging therein critical thinking improve one's ability for effectively fusing together innovation along with effective execution in a real-world context. In direct response to what changes would be made if the interview was to be conducted again; the answer is nothing at all; the overall developed theme and chief hypotheses is considered effective.

Regarding the six step—**reporting and interpretation of data**; it involves the organization of the collective data findings. During this step, all of the essential loose ends are addressed and connected. The main idea is to rightly interpret the data and thus facilitate the results thereof. This critical step determines the overall quality and degree of success pertinent to the comprehensive research study. In direct response to what changes would be made if the interview was to be conducted again; the answer is nothing at all. Hence, the overall quality of the entire interview is considered nothing less than worthy of all the resources invested.

APPENDIX 'A':

Key Participants

The main players who will be involved therein this following interview process includes both the author-researcher Claude E. Bonet, and for the sake of the preservation of anonymity, let us just say that his name is Ian J. Doorighte.

APPENDIX 'B':

Interview Questions

The list of questions considered applicable to the overall interview process is accordingly, in chronological order of facilitation.

1. What initially challenged or provoked you to become a participant in this overall study?

2. What previous experience or knowledge do you have pertinent to the concept of critical thinking?

3. How do you fundamentally define the notion of critical thinking?

4. Please provide a brief real-world example of your first-hand experience where critical thinking was a vital part or aspect.

5. How do you foresee learning the comprehensive intricacies of critical thinking will greatly benefit your career?

6. Do you plan of utilizing critical thinking for your own personal interests or conversely do you eventually plan on becoming a teacher as well?

7. What steps will you utilize in contributing back to the academia which ultimately taught you?

APPENDIX 'C':

Commencement of Transcribed Interview

Welcome **Mr. Doorighte**! I will begin with thanking you for willingly participating in this most important interview. It must be noted that the underlying purpose for this interview is not only for the sake of data or information acquisition, in and of itself, rather most importantly the overall development of a next-generation brand or discipline of critical thinking that is relevant and wholly matured. Anyhow, in regards to your answering the questions presented to you, all that is asked is that you respond to the question as candid and direct as possible. In short, do ensure that the overall context of the information provided is concise, yet fundamentally thorough. Let us now commence.

Interviewer question #1

Mr. Doorighte: what initially challenged or provoked you to become a participant in this overall study? **Doorighte**: I have always been one who understood the importance of both learning and developing critical thinking. That is, critical thinking for me has always been an art-form, as well as a core scientific endeavor. **Interviewer**: I see! In other words, you consider critical thinking as a fundamental part of everyday living. **Doorighte**: That is correct.

Interview question #2

What previous experience or knowledge do you have pertinent to the concept of critical thinking? **Doorighte**: My overall experience goes as far back as my earliest developmental years. In other words, the appreciation and respect that I now possess for critical thinking was instilled by not only my father, but also two teachers whom I encountered, whom by the way were both proud veterans of the US Armed Forces.

Interview question #3

How do you fundamentally define the notion of critical thinking? **Doorighte**: The best way to describe critical thinking as the underlying way of knowing, thinking, and understanding that an individual possesses innately. **Interviewer**: In other words? **Doorighte**: Critical thinking is not about being right or wrong, rather it involves the discovery and identification of novel ideas and notions which beforehand were ignored, overlooked, and/or grossly taken for granted.

Interview statement #1

Please provide a brief real-world example of your first-hand experience where critical thinking was a vital part or aspect. **Doorighte**: The first encounter that I ever had with critical thinking was when I was a mere teen. What transpired what that I feel into a lagoon of water, yet the most unfortunate thing was I had yet learned how to swim, let alone tread water. It was literally a sink or swim; a do or die situation, in which my life was totally depended on my swift adaptation to the situation. **Interviewer**: So it is obvious that were learned rather quickly and succeeded. **Doorighte**: The best way to describe it was I became one with the environment which thus encompassed me. In short, I fused with the water which surrounded me!

Interview question #4

How do you foresee learning the comprehensive intricacies of critical thinking will greatly benefit your career? **Doorighte**: In a nutshell, it will afford a priceless opportunity to not only learn and acquire new and novel information, but also the opportunity to literally reciprocate all that I have already learned and thus mastered, all for the greater good of the collectively germane critical thinking academia. **Interviewer**: it sounds like you understand that critical thinking is more than a meager experience, but also as a process which can never cease to transform. **Doorighte**: Yes, that is correct. I firmly believe in what you might label as the currency of high-level critical thinking. In short, there is such a thing as the *Economics of 360-degree Critical Thinking*^SM.

Interview question #5

Do you plan on utilizing critical thinking for your own personal interests or conversely do you eventually plan on becoming a teacher as well? Like I clearly stated and affirmed in the previous question, the comprehensive process of critical thinking is not completed until the recipient or student thereof has fully given back to the very academic system which generated him or her. Of course, it is the right thing to do! No more and certainly nothing less.

Interview question #6

What steps will you utilize in contributing back to the academia which ultimately taught you? **Doorighte**: the steps that I intend on utilizing includes: 1. Step one-the commitment of remaining actively involved on an ongoing and consistent-basis; 2. Step two-Endeavor to utilize every feasible resource for discovering and uncovering novel and innovative ways for greatly enhancing the overall critical thinking process; Step three-Always maintain the posture of flexibility and having an open-mind; Step four-in the event that I do not know something, I remain willing to ask for assistance and thus acquire new information; Step five-Even as I freely receive new information, I shall likewise freely facilitate and thus offer up vital information.

References

Argyris, C., & Schön, D.A. (1974). *Theory in practice: Increasing professional effectiveness.* San Francisco, CA: Jossey-Bass Publishers.

Booth, W.C., Colomb, G.G., & Williams, J.M. (2008). The craft of research. (3rd ed.). Chicago, IL: The University of Chicago Press.

Brookfield, S.D. (1987). *Developing critical thinkers: Challenging adults to explore alternative ways of thinking and acting.* San Francisco, CA: Jossey-Bass Publishers.

Browne, & Keeley. (1998). *Asking the right questions: A guide to critical thinking.* (5th ed.). Upper Saddle River, NJ: Prentice Hall.

Fisher, D., & Frey, N. (2007). *Checking for understanding: Formative assessment techniques for your classroom.* Alexandria, VA: ASCD.

Jones, W.P. & Kottler, J.A. (2006). *Understanding research: Becoming a competent and critical consumer.* Upper Saddle River, NJ: Pearson-Merrill Prentice Hall.

Lodico, M.G., Spaulding, D.T., & Voegtle, K.H. (2010). *Methods in educational research: From theory to practice.* (2nd ed.). San Francisco, CA: Jossey-Bass.

Marzano, R.J., Waters, T., & McNulty, B.A. (2005). *School leadership that works: From research to results.* Alexandria, VA: ASCD.

McLellan, V. (1978). *Wise words and quotes: An intriguing collection of popular quotes by famous people and wise sayings from scripture.* Wheaton, IL: Tyndale House Publishers, Inc.

ANALYSIS OF STATISTICAL DATA

Abstract

Statistical Analyses affords both researcher and readers the opportunity to assess and critique statistical problems which are identified as common, as well as fundamentally simple. These same problems in fact are required in completion by the educational researcher, regardless if the study's context is qualitative or quantitative. The corresponding problems which are thus afforded needs to be solved, as well as analyzed; pertinent of course to a different aspect of the applicable original data set. As an educational researcher, it is imperative to be able to run similar analyses applicable to any data set. It also includes the data results which were not acquired or gathered, as researchers commonly possess a propensity to collect more data than which is needed and required. In closing, for the sake of not wasting valuable and otherwise vital economy, energy, rigor, and time, the researcher ought to first seek out and thus collect supplemental data sets gathered by colleagues and peers.

Introduction

The "Statistical Analysis: Common Problems and Simple Analyses"; it is a comprehensive, yet succinct critical assessment of statistical problems which are identified as common and simple analyses. It pulls together all of the SPSS/PASW practices from throughout the ED8112—Educational Research Methods course. The chief purpose is to analyze and interpret the final statistical results thereof. Regarding the corresponding tests and calculations: (a) Descriptive Statistics; (b) Crosstabulation and Chi-Square Analyses; (c) T Tests, they are utilized to make inferences about the population based on a sample, commonly referred to as inferential statistics.

Pertinent to the statistical-assessment exercises, the researcher is required to list and provide the generated SPSS/PASW output. The calculated and tabulated results will be formatted in APA style, along with notations and results as indicated within the context of the text instructions. The researcher will provide a 2-3 paragraph summary regarding the results. Each question will be answered exactly as outlined in the text, as well as providing for the instructor specific information asked for in the text. Lastly, regarding the printed output, it is saved into the researcher's computer in MS-Word, utilized for the sake of listing the requisite notations.

Page 104: Descriptive Statistics, Problem #1

Table 7.1. Descriptive Statistics

Full answer provided for students.

	N	Mean	Std. Deviation	Skewness	Kurtosis
ID	105	571366.67	277404.129	-.090	-1.299
GENDER	105	1.39	.490	.456	-1.828
ETHNIC	105	3.35	1.056	-.451	-.554
* YEAR	105	2.94	.691	-.460	.553
LOWUP	105	1.79	.409	-1.448	.099
SECTION	105	2.00	.797	.000	-1.419
* GPA	105	2.7789	.76380	-.052	-.811
EXTRCRED	105	1.21	.409	1.448	.099
REVIEW	105	1.67	.474	-.717	-1.515
* QUIZ1	105	7.47	2.481	-.851	.162
* QUIZ2	105	7.98	1.623	-.656	-.253
X QUIZ3	105	7.98	2.308	-1.134	.750
* QUIZ4	105	7.80	2.280	-.919	.024
* QUIZ5	105	7.87	1.765	-.713	.290
* FINAL	105	61.48	7.943	-.335	-.332
* TOTAL	105	100.57	15.299	-.837	.943
* PERCENT	105	80.34	12.135	-.834	.952
Valid N (list-wise)	105				

Page 114: Cross tabulation and Chi-Square Analyses #1

Table 8.1 GENDER * ETHNICITY Cross tabulation

| | | | ETHNICITY | | | | | |
			1 Native	2 Asian	3 Black	4 White	5 Hispanic	Total
gender	Female	Count	4	13	14	26	7	64
		Expected	3.0	12.2	14.6	27.4	6.7	64.0
		Residual	1.0	.8*	-.6	-1.4	.3*	
	Male	Count	1	7	10	19	4	41
		Expected	2.0	7.8	9.4	17.6	4.3	41.0
		Residual	-1.0*	-.8*	.6	1.4*	-.3	
Total		Count	5	20	24	45	11	105

a 3 cells (30.0%) have expected count less than 5. The minimum expected count is 1.95.

Table 8.1 Chi-Square Tests

	Value	df	Asymp. Sig. (2-sided)
Pearson Chi-Square	1.193	4	<u>.879</u>
			.
Likelihood Ratio	1.268	4	<u>867</u>
Linear-by-Linear Association	.453	1	.501
N of Valid Cases	105		

Table 8.1 Symmetric Measures

		Value	Approx. Sig.
Nominal by	Phi	.107	.879
Nominal	Cramer's V	.107	.879
N of Valid Cases		105	

a   Not assuming the null hypothesis.

b   Using the asymptotic standard error assuming the null hypothesis.

5. Ethnicity and gender are <u>independent</u> of each other.

6. There is no difference of gender balance across different ethnic groups. or, Across different ethnic groups there is no difference in the balance of men and women.

7. No

8. No

9. There are 30% of cells with an expected value of less than 5. Acceptable is less than 25%.

10. Delete the category which most contributes to the low cell counts, the "Native" category in this case.

Page 142: T Tests #1, 2, and 3

Table 11.1 Group Statistics

	gender	N	Mean	Std. Deviation	Std. Error Mean
quiz1	Female	64	7.72	2.306	.288
	Male	41	7.07	2.715	.424
quiz2	Female	64	7.98	1.548	.194
	Male	41	7.98	1.753	.274
quiz3	Female	64	8.19	2.130	.266
	Male	41	7.66	2.555	.399
quiz4	Female	64	8.06	2.181	.273
	Male	41	7.39	2.397	.374
quiz5	Female	64	7.88	1.638	.205
	Male	41	7.85	1.969	.308
final	Female	64	62.36	7.490	.936

Table 11.1 Independent Samples Test

		Levene's Test for Equality of Variances		t-test for Equality of Means					95% Confidence Interval of the Difference	
		F	Sig.	t	df	Sig. (2-tailed)	Mean Difference	Std. Error Difference	Lower	Upper
quiz1	Equal variances assumed	2.180	.143	1.305	103	.195	.646	.495	-.335	1.627
	Equal variances not assumed			1.259	75.304	.212	.646	.513	-.376	1.667
quiz2	Equal variances assumed	1.899	.171	.027	103	.979	.009	.326	-.638	.656
	Equal variances not assumed			.026	77.634	.979	.009	.335	-.659	.676
quiz3	Equal variances assumed	3.436	.067	1.147	103	.254	.529	.461	-.385	1.443
	Equal variances not assumed			1.103	74.189	.274	.529	.480	-.427	1.485
quiz4	Equal variances assumed	.894	.347	1.482	103	.141	.672	.454	-.227	1.572
	Equal variances not assumed			1.452	79.502	.151	.672	.463	-.249	1.594
quiz5	Equal variances assumed	4.103	.045	.060	103	.952	.021	.355	-.682	.725
	Equal variances not assumed			.058	74.071	.954	.021	.369	-.715	.757
final	Equal variances assumed	.093	.761	1.431	103	.156	2.262	1.581	-.874	5.397
	Equal variances not assumed			1.391	77.417	.168	2.262	1.626	-.976	5.500
total	Equal variances assumed	2.019	.158	1.224	103	.224	3.739	3.053	-2.317	9.794
	assumed			1.169	72.421	.246	3.739	3.198	-2.637	1.011E1

No results are statistically significant.

Table 11.2 Paired Samples Statistics

		Mean	N	Std. Deviation	Std. Error Mean
Pair 1	quiz1	7.47	105	2.481	.242
	quiz2	7.98	105	1.623	.158
Pair 2	quiz1	7.47	105	2.481	.242
	quiz3	7.98	105	2.308	.225
Pair 3	quiz1	7.47	105	2.481	.242
	quiz4	7.80	105	2.280	.223
Pair 4	quiz1	7.47	105	2.481	.242
	quiz5	7.87	105	1.765	.172

1. Students scored significantly higher on quiz 2 (M = 7.98, SD = 1.62) than on quiz 1 (M =7.47, SD = (2.48), t(104) = -2.87, p = .005.

2. Students scored significantly higher on quiz 3 (M = 7.98, SD = 2.31) than on quiz 1 (M =7.47, SD = (2.48), t(104) = -4.10, p < .001.

   Notice that the mean values are identical with the first comparison but quiz 1 with quiz 3 pairing produces a much stronger result. This is due to a much narrower standard deviation for the second comparison (1.29) than for the first (1.84)].

3. Students scored significantly higher on quiz 4 (M = 7.80, SD = 1.62) than on quiz 1 (M =7.47, SD = 2.48), t(104) = -2.43, p = .017.

11-3

The values do not differ significantly.

Legend "xxx" = yellow symbolizes data which is circled, as required in original SPSS Output.

"xxx" = blue symbolizes data which is squared, as required in original SPSS Output

Table 11.2 Paired Samples Test

		Paired Differences							
			Std. Error Mean	95% Confidence Interval of the Difference					Sig.
		Std. Deviation		Lower	Upper	t	df		(2-tailed)
		Mean							
Pair 1	quiz1 - quiz2	-.514	1.835	.179	-.869	-.159	-2.872	104	.005
Pair 2	quiz1 - quiz3	-.514	1.287	.126	-.763	-.265	-4.095	104	.000
Pair 3	quiz1 - quiz4	-.333	1.405	.137	-.605	-.061	-2.431	104	.017
Pair 4	quiz1 - quiz5	-.400	2.204	.215	-.827	.027	-1.860	104	.066

ALA—MEASURING CURRENT UNDERSTANDING LEVELS

Abstract

The application of the Adult Learner Assessment (ALA) is; it is an instrument and tool that measures the current level of understanding in which students have navigated and thus matriculated there into. ALA "helps individual college teachers obtain useful feedback on what, how much, and how well their students are learning" (Angelo & Cross, 1993, p. 3). If effectively facilitated, the inevitable result will be the enhanced "effectiveness of many of these decisions by providing more objective information on which to base judgments" (Gronlund & Waugh, 2009, p. 4). Pertinent to its fundamental purpose, it affords both the author and readers alike the opportunity to assess and construct a most necessary learning assessment infrastructure. Hence, the underlying purpose is to construct a theoretically pragmatic framework upon which sound understanding is established and erected thereon. It allows the diverse parties germane to the assessment discuss the overarching concept, as well as the drafting and identification of a threshold-line which ultimately distinguishes the fusion point between the theoretical foundation, as well as the application within a real-world context. Relevant to the systematic correlation existing between instruction and the facilitation of diverse assessments. Moreover, both actually "require that we clearly specify the learning outcomes to be achieved by students, and the provisions of well-designed assessments closely parallel the characteristics of effective instruction" (Gronlund & Waugh, 2009, p. 3). The collective project is sub-divided into three core components; they include: 1. Unit 2—ALA Introduction Draft; 2. Unit 5—ALA Assessment Section Draft; 3. Unit 7—Interpretation of Results Draft; 4. Unit 10—ALA Comprehensive-Final Project, collectively. In a summative nutshell, the main residency-course objective—at the concluding phase or checkpoint—is that the active engager will wholly and successfully develop a summative assessment, appropriate for the full utilization by the germane body of adult student learners.

ALA Introduction Draft

The name of the first section is the ALA Introduction Draft. This section is comprised of the following vital components: 1. Defining the assessment's type and nature; 2. Identifying and explaining the hypothetical learner; 3. Identifying the target learning populations; 4. Identifying at least three learning outcomes to be measured.

Type and Nature of Assessment

The overarching category-type under which the assessment is identified is called Authentic Assessments. This specific type measures students' current level of understanding, as well as the relevance to resolving real world challenges and issues. It concentrates on "real-life tasks"; it also "stresses the importance of focusing on the application of understandings and skills" (Gronlund & Waugh, 2009, p 2) applicable to pragmatic contextual situations. It is considered a most effective way to determine if students are prepared to function and navigate within the real world.

Identify & Explain the Hypothetical Learner—Target Population

The hypothetical learner includes students within the age range of eighteen to thirty-five, aka Generation-Y, and The Millenials. These students possess educational experience ranging from right out of high school up to and including graduate-level studies. They originate from diverse socio-cultural, economic, and religious backgrounds. The economic-statuses include part-time status, full-time status; entrepreneurial status plus self-made millionaires. In short, this is a collective group assembled under the chief principle entitled holistic quasi-cultural engagement.

Identify the Hypothetical Subject

The hypothetical subject is called Critical Thinking. It is an academic discipline which typically falls under the collective field of Professional and Human Development. It is established upon the core teaching philosophy which affirms that if students are gathered together from vastly diverse parts of the globe, the probability for next-dimension critical thinking is greatly enhanced and increased. As a direct result, the collective student body consequentially matriculates into a distinct class of effective and matured analytical-critical thinkers. It is, in short, a novel theoretical framework called Quantum Acad(yna^{E3})mics^{SM}, a three-phased residency which concentrates upon the collective fusing together of innovation and active execution.

Identification of the Core Learning Objectives

The first objective, Unit 1—Exactly Why Am I Participating—Underlying Motivations, is comprised of three instructional learning tenets:

1. Critically assess, examine, and investigate one's underlying motivations—personal and professional.
2. Identify and critically discuss the importance, as well as its relevance to the real-world.
3. Assess the definition of wisdom, and make it applicable to one's individual context.

The second objective, Unit 2—What is Critical Thinking—Fundamental Intricacies, is comprised of four instructional tenets:

1. Grasp firm understanding of the basics of the brain and cognitive functioning.
2. Understand the direct correlation between mastering one's brain and becoming an effective critical thinker.
3. Be able to skillfully and successfully discuss the quasi-dimensional facets of this subject.
4. Develop a balanced and effective argument. Attempt to persuade others pertinent to one's philosophy & novel viewpoint.

In short, if any student is to navigate and matriculate through residency, he or she must first both acquire and master the critical thinking rudimentary.

ALA Section Draft

The second section is called the ALA Section Draft. The section's main purpose is to afford all parties involved the opportunity to critically assess the intricacies of the actual testing assessment instrument. It includes directions intended for the corresponding administers, plus those taking the assessment; it is comprised of the following sub-sections:

1. Section one, which is divided into two fundamental parts, requires the description of the course, and the design of the actual assessment instrument; it is developed for utilization within the final course project.
2. Section two requires the allocation or provision of directions for both the assessment administrator, as well as the target students engaged in the assessment.
3. Section three requires a description regarding how special needs students will be accommodated.
4. Section four requires the design of the assessment items that are linked to the learning objectives.

5. Section five requires that the assessment item types being matched to the skills being assessed.

6. Section six requires that the design of the assessment consistent regarding the specific context of the learning environment in which it is applicable.

Brief Course Description

This course is designed and engineered upon an overarching concept dubbed by the author as the Hyper-meta Cognition^SM Theoretical Learning Model it is the plane of critical and analytical thinking where the next-dimension of progressive critical analysis-thinking transpires. The chief premise upon which the residency concept is established is that it is the highest-level of consistently unparalleled critical facilitates thereon. It is a next-dimension realm of critical thinking, where the following two distinct aspects: 1. Ongoing critical thinking; 2. Intuitive critical reflection, are both fused together. The official name of this course is QCAD 1501.E1, the "Clay & Pine" Phase; it is fundamentally comprised of the following two core components:

1. Unit 1—Exactly Why Am I Participating: Underlying Motivations?
2. Unit 2—What is Critical Thinking: Fundamental Intricacies?

The first unit's learning objective affords deeper insights into the undergirding motivations behind the student enrolling in this residency. The second unit's learning objective involves acquiring the basic essentials of critical thinking. In short, at the conclusion of this residency, the student will have participated in real-world case scenarios, created-applied solution plans, demonstrated mastery of learning program intricacies, and effectively presented and defended applicable arguments.

Learning Environment & Accommodating Special Need Students

The critical thinking process which occurs within the context of this residency is similar to the research and development prevalent within most scientific research laboratories;

every interaction is contained and controlled. The facilitation of information is described as a "face-to-face" learning contextual setting.

Pertinent to accommodating students with special needs, the assessment administrators are required to afford as much accommodation as possible. This also includes the extension of required taking time, the assistance in receiving the requisite resources-tools and logistics relevant to taking the assessment. In short, it involves the necessary finishing of the assessment, as well as the ultimate departure from the premises.

Instructions for the Testing Administrator

Each question is categorized under the specific unit in which it applies, as identified within the corresponding brackets. The specific unit in which the question or item applies can be found with brackets. Before commencing, the administrator is required to facilitate instructions, as well as remain available for questions which might arise during the session.

ALA Interpretation of Results Draft

The third and final section is called the ALA Interpretation of Results Draft. The main purpose for this section is to provide insights into the utilization and measuring thereof, germane to the performance-level of students-learners. Hence, these assessments "help individual college teachers obtain useful feedback on what, how much, and how well their students are learning" (Angelo & Cross, 1993, p. 3). Assessments assist educators in shifting the direction of their teaching; serving "to help students make their learning more efficient" (Angelo & Cross, 1993, p. 3). Through the administration of diverse principles-practices, greater contribution is afforded to "more effective classroom instruction and improved student learning" (Gronlund & Waugh, 2009, p. v). In sum, it is an integral part of the comprehensive teaching-learning process.

Development of the Assessment and Utilization

The overarching assessment type of this assignment is the authentic assessment. The authentic assessment is "a title for performance assessments that stresses the importance of focusing on the application of understanding and skills to real problems in 'real world' contextual settings" (Gronlund & Waugh, 2009, p. 2).

Regarding both the actual assessment sub-types, and tabulated results, it is triple-tiered. At the course's onset, students are provided a placement assessment; it determines entry-level performance. It addresses a "singular area of concentration": 1. Readiness concern—at the course onset, do the students possess the basic or requisite rudimentary skills? After the course has begun, students are tested in a manner reflective of the formative assessment. This type monitors learning progress. Towards the course's conclusion, students are administered a summative assessment. This type, in fact, is utilized "to determine terminal performance" (Gronlund & Waugh, 2009, pp. 9-10). The next step involves the implementation of fundamental core components; it is divided into four main categories. The actual structural layout is sub-divided into three core sub-sections: 1. True/False; 2. Multiple Choice; 3. Essay Questions.

The comprehensive assessment is an assignment draft that assesses, and measures: 1. Aptitude; 2. Performance-level, and; 3. Overall understanding. The chief purpose thereof is to tabulate the target student body's understanding pertinent to the underlying motivation for enrolling in the course, and the subsequent active participating. It delves into the vital insights of the fundamental intricacies of critical thinking; how to tap into and unleash dormant abilities, and the direct application, as well as relevance within a real world context.

This name of the course is QCAD 1501.E1, the 'Clay & Pine' Phase. It is designed and engineered upon the overarching concept dubbed as the Hyper-meta Cognition^SM Theoretical Learning Model. The course's chief premise is that there is such a realm in which the highest-level of critical functioning, reasoning, and thinking occurs therein. It is a next-dimension realm of critical thinking, where the following two distinct aspects: 1. Ongoing critical thinking; 2. Intuitive critical reflection, are synergistically fused together.

Interpretation and Grading of Assessment

Professors Gronlund and Waugh (2009) affirm that the "main purpose of a classroom assessment plan is to improve student learning" (p. 19). The most effective testing assessments are facilitated in the following sequential order: 1. Instruction; 2. Achievement Domain; 3. Achievement Assessment (Gronlund & Waugh, 2009, p. 21). It provides: 1. Relative ranking of students; 2. Description of the learning tasks a student can and cannot perform (Gronlund & Waugh, 2009, p. 24). Concerning the motivation for finding the right assessment, it literally begins and ends at the point in which students are equipped for becoming capable, competent, and effective individuals.

Angelo and Cross (1993) divulge that "helping students learn the subject matter of their courses is the most common goal of college teachers, and virtually all teachers try to measure what students are learning about the content being taught" (p. 106). There are two basic methods for assessment interpretation, the norm-referenced assessment type, and the criterion-referenced assessment type. The specific type utilized in this context is criterion-referenced. Both teachers and students are afforded snapshots into the motivation behind student involvement, as well as sound understanding of the core critical thinking intricacies.

The faculty and student body will master the essentials for tapping into and unleashing the set of dormant abilities—critical thinking powers within, as well as identifying a clear link between critical thinking as a concept-discipline and its pragmatic relevance. All of which directly corresponds to the application within a real world situational context. Regarding the chief basis for grading, it is of the absolute grading style. That is "letter grades are typically assigned by comparing a student's performance to a prespecified standard of performance"; it is a common type of grading system that "utilizes letter grades defined by a 100-point system (Gronlund & Waugh, 2009, p. 192. It is the preferred method of traditional learning institutions.

Assessment Grading Instrument-Rubric

The main objective for the grading rubric is to assess the student's foundational mastery of the course, as well as the conceptual context. The measured rubric elements are classified into "seven rudimentary categories". The grading rubric categories addressed, includes:

1. Efficacy of APA Format-Style;
2. Organization of Ideas and Thoughts;
3. Breadth and Depth of Ideas and Insights;
4. Ability to identify and articulate relevance to real world context;
5. Stability of foundation via mechanical and sentence structure.
6. Multiple Choice Questions;
7. True/False Questions.

The overall purpose for the rubric is the utilization towards to the guiding and navigation throughout the comprehensive assessment process. It directly responds to the questions, such as: 1. Have the course objectives have been mastered; 2. What specific degree of supplemental training is deemed warranted. The rubric is facilitated on three different occasions during each corresponding training course-workshop. The overall content of the course correlates directly to the specific assessment being facilitated.

The rubric's overall quality is considered valid and reliable. The chief justification as to why the rubric is considered as valid is because the results "provide a representative and relevant measure of the achievement domain under consideration" (Gronlund & Waugh, 2009, p. 46). In direct response to why the rubric is considered, thus deemed reliable, it is because regardless of how many times it is taken, consistency in the overall official results tabulated occurs. Professors Oermann & Gaberson (2009) confirm that "scoring rubrics work well for assessing papers" (p. 235). The assessment rubric assesses and validates the following unit components:

1. Why Am I Participating: Underlying Motivations;
2. What is Critical Thinking: Fundamental Intricacies;

3. Diving Right In, Becoming Actively Engaged;

4. Application of Course Knowledge in Real World Context: How Will I Benefit & Measured Development.

In short, regardless of the frequency of assessment facilitation, plus the utilization of diverse yet equal sample items, the results are consistent.

Conclusion and Final Reflections

The overall and encompassing conclusion pertinent to this application of the Adult Learner Assessment (ALA) is that an instrument or tool that measures the current level of understanding in which students have navigated and thus matriculated into. The collective ALA project is sub-divided into three core components. The overarching category-type under which the assessment is identified is called Authentic Assessments; it measures students' current level of understanding, as well as the relevance to resolving real world challenges and issues. The hypothetical learner includes students within the age range of eighteen to thirty-five, aka Generation-Y, and The Millenials. The name of the hypothetical subject is Critical Thinking; it is an academic discipline which categorized under collective field called Professional and Human Development.

Pertinent to the core learning objectives, there are two: 1. Unit 1—Exactly Why Am I Participating—Underlying Motivations; 2. Unit 2—What is Critical Thinking—Fundamental Intricacies. The name of the second section is the Section Draft. The section's main purpose is to afford all parties involved the opportunity to critically assess the intricacies of the actual testing assessment instrument. The collective residency-course is designed and engineered upon a concept referred to as the Hyper-meta Cognition^{SM} Theoretical Learning Model, the plane in which next-dimension of progressive critical analysis-thinking transpires.

The critical thinking process which occurs is similar to the research and development prevalent within a vast majority of scientific research laboratories. Each question is categorized under the specific unit in which it applies, as identified within a corresponding set of brackets. Learning assessments are used to test and measure the performance-level of students-learners. The overarching assessment type of this comprehensive final project is aptly named the ***Authentic Assessment***. There are two basic methods for assessment interpretation, the norm-referenced assessment type, and the criterion-referenced assessment type.

Regarding the chief basis for grading, it is of the absolute grading style. In closing, the main objective for the grading rubric is to assess the student's foundational mastery of the course, as well as the conceptual context. The rubric's overall quality is considered valid and reliable. Thus, regardless of the frequency of assessment facilitation, as well as the utilization of diverse yet equal sample items, the results are consistent and unwavering.

Lastly, for the sake of addressing and thus responding to the key final question, how the process of interpreting assessments can have an impact on your teaching, the summative-response is as follows. If nothing else, for starters, the individual(s) will be better equipped at interpreting learning-teaching assessments. That is a firm, sound, and unwavering foundational understanding will be thoroughly established. Fisher and Frey (2007) citing Lapp et al. reveals that the "following four reasons tests and assessments are commonly used:

1. Diagnosing individual student needs;
2. Informing instruction;
3. Evaluating programs;
4. Providing accountability information (2001, p. 7; p. 100).

In other words, it affords the corresponding parties the necessary information—resources and tools—for drafting and thus facilitation an vitally essential assessing framework which "provides the roadmap for the integration of face-to-face and online activities" (Garrison and Vaughan, 2008, p. 3). Hence, the underlying point is that it firmly sets and establishes the necessary learning-teaching assessment infrastructure upon which the official measuring and gathering of otherwise vital information derived from vastly diverse cultures and backgrounds can be accomplished.

Thus, a blended community of learning-teaching inquiry can successfully and wholly be completed, from start to finish; it is through and most comprehensive. Hence, the ability to interpret learning-teaching assessments, it positions-postures the applicable assessment team with the chief purpose of engaging therein the "process of gathering information from multiple sources and indicators to make judgments about student learning, achievement, progress, and performance" (Branche et al. citing Frey, 2007, p. 23). In short, the assessment administrator or facilitator is thoroughly equipped in assessing, measuring, and tabulating the overall ability and competence—past and present—of the target and germane student body to the results, as well as seceding actions thereof, whom will otherwise benefit, regardless of positively or negatively.

References

Angelo, T.A., & Cross, K.P. (1993). *Classroom assessment techniques: A handbook for college teachers*. (2nd ed.). San Francisco, CA: John Wiley & Sons, Inc.

Branche, J., Mullennix, J., & Cohn, E.R. (2007). *Diversity across the curriculum: A guide for faculty in higher education*. San Francisco, CA: Jossey-Bass.

Brookfield, S.D. (1995). *Becoming a critically reflective teacher*. San Francisco, CA: Jossey-Bass.

Brookfield, S.D. (1987). *Developing critical thinkers: Challenge adults to explore alternative ways of thinking and acting*. San Francisco, CA: Jossey-Bass Publishers.

Garrison, D.R., & Vaughan, N.D. (2007). *Blended learning in higher education: Framework, principles, and guidelines*. San Francisco, CA: Jossey-Bass.

Gronlund, N.E., & Waugh, C.K. (2009). *Assessment of student achievement*. (9th ed.). Upper Saddle River, NJ: Pearson-Merrill.

Oermann, M.H., & Gaberson, K.B. (2009). *Evaluation and testing in nursing education*. (3rd ed.). New York, NY: Springer.

Paul, R., & Elder, L. (2006). *Critical thinking: Tools for taking charge of your learning and your life*. (2nd ed.). Upper Saddle River, NJ: Pearson-Prentice Hall.

The Jossey-Bass Reader. (2007). *Educational leadership*. (2nd ed.). San Francisco, CA: John Wiley & Sons, Inc.

APPENDIX 'A':

Instructions for the Students

Students are required to thoroughly read the specific directions which correlates to the sub-section. If any questions or issue of concern arises, the student is encouraged to notify any one of the listed and designated test facilitators present during the administration of the assessment test.

Assessment Instrument

The following assessment test is intended to critically assess, as well as evaluate—measure and tabulate—the target body of students understanding of the underlying motivation for their enrolling in the course, the fundamental intricacies of critical thinking, how to tap into and unleash dormant abilities, and the direct application plus relevance into a real world context.

Target-Subject Population:

Generation 'Y' (Gen-Y), aka The Millenials. These are students that fall within the age range of 18 thru 35.

Core Subject:

Critical thinking and its application within a real world situational context; it is established upon the overarching concept called the Hyper-meta Cognition™® Theoretical Learning Model.

Structural Layout of Assessment:

The test assessment is sub-divided into three core sub-sections—

1. True or False questions (5);
2. Multiple Choice questions (10);
3. Essays questions (2).

Disclaimer Notice: the number within the parenthesis identifies the exact number of items comprised within that distinct assessment-section.

Section One—True or False [Unit 1 & Unit 2]

The following questions are to be answered based upon current understanding of what is true or false. The only requirement circle the most correct or singular response. Notice, the correct answer is found within the parenthesis.

1. One of the chief result of learning critical thinking and the effective application thereof is because it is a productive and positive activity (Brookfield, 1987, p. 5)? (True)
2. The comprehensive learning of critical thinking can result in a greater or higher level of both imagining and the exploration of alternatives (Brookfield, 1987, p. 8)? (True)
3. Learning critical thinking essentially makes one a less competent professional (Brookfield, 1987, p. 12)? (False)
4. One of the greatest benefits of learning critical thinking is that it will ultimately result in my becoming a more successful individual—personally and professionally (Brookfield, 1987, p. 43). (True)
5. Does each individual have the innate ability to tap into and fully develop critical thinking skills (The Jossey-Bass Reader, 2007, p. 7)? (True)

Section Two—Multiple Choice [Unit 2]

Each underlined section corresponds to an answer choice. The first underlined section corresponds to choice 'A'. Kindly select the answer choice that is considered the most accurate answer:

1. Which of the following is a motivation for learning critical thinking (Brookfield, 1995, p. 28)?
   - A. I Have Nothing Else to Do
   - B. I Am Disinterested in Business Administration
   - C. Arriving at a Place of Awareness is a Puzzling Task
   - D. To Have a Certificate To Hang Upon the Wall

2. How will taking critical thinking improve my relationship with my colleagues and peers (Brookfield, 1995, p. 28)?
   - A. Attempting to Understand My Colleagues-Peers is otherwise a Daunting Task
   - B. I Will Become Better Equipped in Manipulating Others
   - C. I Will Have the Upper Hand in Applying for a Promotion
   - D. It Will Teach Me to Become Telepathic

3. How does learning and mastering critical thinking improve my ability to teach (Brookfield, 1995, p. 39)?
   - A. I Have Another Credential to Add To My Resume'
   - B. I am Better Apt in Naming & Confronting Dilemmas Plus Contradiction
   - C. More People Will Be Impressed By My Abilities
   - D. I Am Now More Competitive For Attaining Higher Paying Promotions

4. Critical reflection is a matter of which of the following (Brookfield, 1995, p. 42)?
   - A. Stance and Dance
   - B. Flight or Fight
   - C. Shuck and Jive
   - D. Ask and Inquire

5. What does it mean to speak authentically (Brookfield, 1995, p. 45)?

    A. Have a Voice of Persuasion

    B. To Become a More Effective Communicator

    C. To Say What I Mean and Mean What I Say

    D. Alert to the Voices within That Are Not Our Own

6. Which of the following is an important facet of helping people to think critically (Brookfield, 1987, p. 78)?

    A. To Become Vice President of their Organization

    B. To Be Undefeated at Playing Chess

    C. Provide Them an Opportunity to Undertake Periods of Reflective Evaluations

    D. To Learn How to Paint Like Rembrandt

7. According to Gamson & Associates, the Process of Engaging Students for Critical Awareness is best defined as (Brookfield, 1987, p. 80):

    A. Liberating Education

    B. Ought to Be a Degree Program Offered at the University

    C. An Extracurricular Activity

    D. A Process That is Ongoing and Never-ending

8. In reference to the Stages of Development of critical thinking, which of the following is identified as the fourth stage (Paul & Elder, 2006, p. 26)?

    A. Master Thinker

    B. Apathetic Thinker

    C. Hyperactive Thinker

    D. Practicing Thinker

9. Which of the following statements best understood as a summation of critical thinking (Paul & Elder, 2006, p. xvii)?

    A. A Computer Component

    B. Art of Thinking about Thinking

    C. A Pharmaceutical Drug

    D. A Meditative Posture

10. Good thinking requires which of the following (Paul & Elder, 2006, p. xx)?

    A. Hard Work

    B. Vitamin B-12

    C. Unwavering Commitment

    D. A Great Pair of Running Shoes

Section Three—Essay Questions [Unit 1 & Unit 2]

Students are required to answer the following questions as directly and concise as possible. In fact, the answers should directly correlate with identified or recognized common knowledge within the academic discipline or field of critical thinking.

1. Since enrolling in this course, how have you become more effective in resolving issues on your job?

2. Have you experienced greater positive feedback from your colleagues and peers concerning your ability or relate to and understand others?

Appendix 'B'

Final Project Rubric:

Criteria	Non-performance	Basic	Inter-mediate	Distinguish	Worthy of Being a Mentor—Sage-level	Total Points Accumulated
APA Format-Style (60 pts.)	No evidence of APA fundamentals <22	Demonstrates basics of APA 30 28 26 24 22	Good utilization of APA strategy & techniques 38 36 34 32	Demonstrates advanced knowledge of APA strategy & techniques 46 44 42 40	Is effective enough to facilitate APA training unto others in training environment/setting 60 58 56 54	?
Organization of Ideas and Thoughts (40 pts.)	Ideas and Thoughts are incoherent, illogical, and nonsensical <10	Ideas and Thoughts reflective of one with basic understanding of communication 16 14 12 10	Ideas and thoughts reflective of one whom understands influence and persuasion 24 22 20 18	Ideas and thoughts reflective of one highly gifted communicator 32 30 28 26	Ideas and thoughts reflective of master communicator, one qualified to mentor, teach, and train others 40 38 36 34	?
Breadth and Depth of Ideas and Insights (50 pts.)	The ideas and insights presented have little to no substance <20	The ideas and insight have basic foundation 26 24 22 20	The ideas and insights are reflective of one with substance; it is logical, and eye catching 34 32 30 28	The ideas and insights are reflective of a person with high-level ability, skills, and knowledge 42 40 38 36	The ideas and insights are reflective of an individual whom is high-level critical thinker, innovative and ought to train others how to think and express self 50 48 46 44	?
Ability to identify and articulate relevance to real world context (70 pts.)	Information articulated does not make sense; it is difficult to understand <40	Basic skills in articulating information 46 44 42 40	Demonstrates high-level skills in link information with real world context 54 52 50 48	Advanced ability and skills in drafting link between pertinent information and real world 62 60 58 56	Demonstrates such command of drafting link with real world that ought to teach and train others 70 68 66 64	?
Stability of foundation via	No evidence of the	Facilitates knowledge	Facilitates knowledge	Facilitates knowledge	Is so highly effective and skills at written	

mechanical and sentence structure (50 pts.)	rudimentary and foundational intricacies understood <20	in a manner that demonstrated a basic foundation 26 24 22 20	in a manner of one that is gifted and skills at communication and expression; firm foundation and beyond 34 32 30 28	as one that is highly advanced and have mastered written communication 42 40 38 36	communication that ought to be teaching and training others 50 48 46 44	?
Multiple Choice Questions (35 pts.)	Demonstrates no understanding of critical thinking (<25% correct) <11	Demonstrates basic or little understanding of critical thinking (>25%; <50% correct) 17 15 13 11	Demonstrates considerable understanding of critical thinking (>50 %; <75% correct) 25 23 21 19	Demonstrates advance knowledge and understanding of critical thinking (>75 % correct) 33 31 29 27	Demonstrates such high-level ability, worthy of teaching and training others (100% correct) 35	?
True/False Questions (20 pts.)	No response/ task not attempted (0% correct) <8	Demonstrates basic understanding of critical thinking 10 8	Demonstrates high-level understanding of critical thinking 14 12	Demonstrates advance-level understanding of critical thinking 18 16	Demonstrates complete understanding of critical thinking; ought to be teaching and training others 20	?

Scores:

Section 1—APA Format-Styles (60 possible points)

Section 2—Organization of Ideas and Thoughts (40 possible points)

Section 3—Breadth and Depth of Ideas and Insights (50 possible points)

Section 4—Ability to identify, articulate relevance to real world context

(70 possible points)

Section 5—Stability of foundation via mechanical and sentence structure

(50 possible points)

Section 6—Multiple Choice Questions (35 possible points)

Section 7—True/False Questions (20 possible points)

   Total possible points to accrue@ **[325 points]**

Points and Letter Grade Correlation Scale:

Notice-Instead of listing or categorizing as "collective tabulated points", the grading scale is instead identified in percentile-form.

For example, an A$^+$ would range—hypothetically speaking—between 1200 (100%; minimum) points to 1176 (98%; maximum) points; the total points which can be accrued over the length of the residency tabulates at 1200 total points.

100-98	A$^+$	80-78 C$^+$	≤60	F
97-94	A	77-74 C		
93-91	A$^-$	73-71 C$^-$		
90-88	B$^+$	70-68 D$^+$		
87-84	B	67-64 D		
83-81	B$^-$	63-61 D$^-$		

ADDITIONAL-PERTINENT ARTICLE

Institutional Servant Leadership
Focus of the Research or Hypothesis:

The fundamental focus of Brian C. Grizzell's research is the deductive assessment of the constructive ramifications of "Servant leadership". In other words, readers are afforded an objectively-unbiased insight into the critical link between servant leadership—at the grassroots level, and the longevity of a healthy communal life. Brian C. Grizzell affirms "This paper is a critical essay that discusses the influence of servant leadership on urban community sustainability" (2008, p. 1).

In addition, it provides objective analyses into what has already been implemented, as well as the eradication of "chronically destructive" behaviors, all within an urban communal context. The practices utilized, in fact, occur at both the "individual-level" and the "corporate-level" or institutional-level (p. 1).

Used by Researcher:

The focus is achieved through the utilization of diverse investigative techniques, including word-of-mouth, reflective journals, articles, and essays. It is also achieved through the information gathered from community-partnerships. A brief list of communication channel examples includes Dr. Ronald Mason's statement regarding the "grassroots benefactor of servant leadership", Robin Kelley's statement regarding the migration of "upward mobile individuals to the suburbs"; Hence, Greenleaf's statement concerning servant leadership, in essence being a *shared leadership model.*

Next, there is Smiley's suggestion "to strengthen the ability of community members to have input on healthy living decisions affecting them; to increase advocacy skills building, and to actively change the community in its well-being" (Grizzell, 2008, pp. 3-4). In summary, the information gathered was achieved via the researchers' actively, thus proactively engaging into diverse avenues of communication.

Peter G. Northouse (2007) asserts that the five dimensions of the trait theory approach are intelligence, self-confidence, determination, integrity, and sociability (p. 19). S. Truett Cathy; he is the lone founder and chairman of Chick-fil-A, and a esteemed plus recognized national leader who demonstrates and personifies the *trait theory approach* to leadership.

S. Truett Cathy; he is a leader who consistently demonstrates intelligence by "concocting a boneless chicken breast on a buttered bun" while his major competitors focused rather upon conventional hamburgers (Kennedy, J. 2008, p. 52). It was a decision which paid off. Mr. Cathy also demonstrates sociability by his commitment towards mentoring future leaders. He affirms that his restaurants are mere "vehicles to produce good citizens as well as profits" (p. 53).

S. Truett Cathy; he is a leader who also demonstrates self-confidence. He is self-assured in making otherwise risky decisions. For example, "when other businesses started opening on Sundays to create more cash flow, he kept the doors to his restaurants shut tight" (p. 52). Mr. Cathy also demonstrates both integrity and determination by remaining true to his belief that, "People and principles" come before profit (p. 53).

In summary, Mr. S. Truett Cathy; he is irrefutably an extremely intelligent, sociable, self-confident, determined, and last yet not least of all, a man of unwavering integrity. These traits are exemplified by Mr. Cathy's willingness to take a risk, his commitment in mentoring future leaders of society, his self-assurance in pursuing risky ventures, his placing people before profits, and finally his willingness in taking time to better the quality of life for others. For S. Truett Cathy is without a doubt a national leader who both demonstrates and personifies the trait theory approach to leadership in action.

References

Kennedy, J. (2008, July). God's Billionaire. U.S. News & World Report, Collector's Edition, 52-53.

Northouse, P.G. (2007). *Leadership theory and practice*. (4th ed.). Thousand Oaks, CA: SAGE Publications.

LEADER-MEMBER EXCHANGE THEORY

The Leader-Member Exchange Theory; it is a leadership theory which encompasses and likewise is firmly erected and established upon the premise of the necessity for exchange-transaction of resources. Peter G. Northouse (2006) divulges that the theory is a dyadic-relationship modality "centered on the interactions between leaders and followers" (p. 151). In brief, the theory can improve leadership effectiveness within *LA Fitness Center* by describing leadership and prescribing leadership.

Next, the description of leadership is achieved by identifying the current paradigm, and hence applying in relevance to the relationship with followers. Leadership is offered valuable insights for improving this behavioral-communicative process. Furthermore, leadership involves the dyadic relationship between the leader and his followers. Northouse (2006) reveals that the "LMX theory is noteworthy because it directs our attention to the importance of communication in leadership" (p. 159).

The prescription of leadership, moreover, is achieved by assisting managers in rightly assessing from a *relationship perspective*. It affords information into how networks are constructed. This is achieved by addressing and resolving the vast possible complexities involved. Leaders are given understanding into the "what and why" of human motivation. Professor Northouse asserts, "A person with a network of high-quality partnerships can call on many people to help solve problems and advance the goals of the organization" (p. 162).

In summary, LA Fitness Center can experience leadership effectiveness by describing leadership and prescribing leadership. It is a process which is achieved by the application of the Leadership-Member Exchange Theory—a dyadic theory which encompasses the exchange-transaction of resources between a leader and his followers.

Essay Discussion:

Describe how the careful plus highly methodical *application* of the Leader-Member Exchange Theory could improve leadership effectiveness in an organization with which you are very familiar.

Although the invention has been explained in relation to its preferred embodiment, it is to be understood that many other possible modifications and variations can be made without departing from the spirit and scope of the invention as hereinafter claimed.

REVISIT OF NECESSITY FOR FACILITATING THE QUANTUM SYSTEM

The world in which we live is swiftly changing right before our very eyes. Just within the past decade, there has been intensifying national debate pertaining to America's dire need for ending its dependence upon fuel reserves derived from "oil-gas producing" Middle Eastern countries. The chief international conglomerate which facilitates the distribution of these reserves is commonly referred to as the Organization of the Petroleum Exporting Countries (OPEC). OPEC was first developed in 1960—Baghdad, Iraq, with its main function serving to "regulate oil production, and thereby manage oil prices, in a coordinated effort among the member countries" ("OPEC", 2004). Cremer and Weitzman (2002) corroborates that OPEC is essentially "viewed as a monopolist sharing the oil market with a competitive sector". The oil conglomerate is thus comprised of the following core nations:

1. Algeria;
2. Indonesia;
3. Iran;
4. Iraq;
5. Kuwait;
6. Libya;
7. Nigeria;
8. Qatar;
9. Saudi Arabia;
10. United Arab Emirates, and;
11. Venezuela ("OPEC", 2004).

Appreciative Inquiry Precept

Existing at the nucleus of this ongoing debate is the need to: 1. design; 2. develop, and; 3. implement alternative methods for which this endeavor can become a manifested reality. It requires, in fact, the active and unwavering commitment of its leaders and delegated "powers-that-be" to engage in a series of much needed *think tank-driven sessions*.

A prime example of the type of discourse that will contribute greatly towards the overall outcome is the "Appreciative Inquiry (AI) Model". Hence, Preskill and Catsambas (2006) aver that AI is defined as "a group process that inquires into, identifies, and further develops the best of 'what is' in organizations in order to create a better future" (p. 1).

Two Fundamental Components

Next, it "helps align evaluation activities with an organization's mission and performance goals" (Preskill & Catsambas, 2006, p. 99). It consists of two fundamental components: 1. "4-D Model"; 2. "4-I Model". Also, the 4-D consists of four phases: 1. Discovering; 2. Dreaming; 3. Designing; 4. Destiny. Likewise, the 4-I consists of four phases: 1. Inquire; 2. Imagine; 3. Innovate; 4. Implement (Preskill, 2006, p. 8, slides 15-16). In short, AI affords the relevant decision making parties the requisite particulars for ensuring that the required energy, resources, and time invested produces, in the end, quantified-dividends.

Pragmatic Relevancy

Nevertheless, pertinent to the underlying thread which runs throughout the length and breadth of this course project, it requires that two fundamentally core components exist: 1. Innovation, and; 2. Execution. Thus, the main reason as to why innovation and execution are considered essential components, plus core elements is because they are considered as the chief pillars upon which the comprehensive critical thinking (CT) system irrefutably exists thereon.

Hence, in order for the totality of CT to materialize—start to finish, creative innovation must immediately (double-underscored) be followed by unfaltering and unprecedented action-execution. Brookfield (1987) echoes this sentiment with affirming that "We have seen that critical thinking comprises two interrelated processes: identifying and challenging assumptions, and imagining and exploring alternatives" (p. 229). In other words, innovation that is not followed with immediate execution often results in utter-total failure.

According to The New International Webster's Standard Dictionary (2006) in fact innovation is defined as "n. something new; the process of introducing something new" (p. 151). Execution, on the other hand is understood as the necessary steps that an entity—individual, organizational, or otherwise, must effectuate or engage therein so that the desired results will consequentially result. It is defined as "n. 1. The state or process of acting or doing; 2. A movement or series of movements; 3. Habitual or vigorous activity; energy" ("American Heritage Dictionary", 1994, p. 8).

Hence, the distinct difference between both ideas is that innovation fundamentally involves intense reflection, thought, and debate, whereas execution is nothing less than the application, facilitation, and implementation of all that has been thoroughly discussed.

"Quantum Acad(yna^{E3})mics^{SM}: Critical Thinking, The Vital Agent Which Fuses Innovation with Execution" is a hypothetical, yet ever-developing extreme-workshop that will eventually be utilized in a real-world context. It affords its residency-students (student body) several opportunities to research, assess, and investigate current theories and real world cases. It affords the opportunity, moreover, to reconstruct and reinvent the most prevalent current ways of thinking. It focuses thereon the growth and development of one's ability to engage in comprehensive CT; it is a concept called "Meta-cognition"—the comprehensive ongoing and cyclical critiquing of critical thinking. It endeavors to identify "explanations of individual differences in cognition" (Roberts & Ardos, 2010, "Abstract" Section).

Conclusion

In closing, it is considered as "central to planning, problem-solving, evaluation and many aspects of language learning" (Kearsley, 2004-2010, "Introduction" Section). In a nutshell, the workshop focuses thereon CT as the vital agent which fuses together the elements of innovation with execution. As a direct result, there will be the successful matriculation of a class of unparalleled thinkers whom are highly effective, highly skilled, and most competent agents of sociocultural, socioeconomic, and sociopolitical change.

REFLECTIVE ACADEMICS MATRICULATION

Abstract

Reflective Academics Matriculation; perhaps the most effective method for rightly describing this current and most prevalent theory-in-action. Argyris and Schön (1974) reveals that it is fundamentally, "the integration of thought with action" (p. 3). Hence, it is that precise moment when the theory or "set of interconnected propositions that have the same referent "becomes fused with the application, or pragmatic implementation of that same theoretical knowledge (Argyris and Schön, 1974, pp. 3-5).

What exactly is reflective academics matriculation? It is sort of like a digital camera—perhaps a Nikon D90 SLR Digital Camera, for example. It possesses what is referred to as panoramic capabilities. Thus, this camera has the ability to capture an image, person, object, or event from a vastly broad angle or "frame-of-reference". In brief, the main or chief purpose for this discussion is to reflect how the overarching theory directly influences one's decision to enroll in any higher education or certification learning setting. The formula is simply: Every *consequence* 'C' is directly influenced by a precise *action or set of actions* 'A' which directly corresponds to an encompassing *situation* 'S'.

Moment of Personal Reflection

As I reflect and attempt to draft the vast wealth of thought into this literary memo, I honestly exist at the threshold of three realities. **Reality one**; is the precipice of the past which connects to the corridor called the second reality. **Reality two**; the corridor of facing the present or current circumstances head-on. **Reality three**; the successful matriculation of my doctoral students and its direct influence upon the complete and total completion of this innovative strategic system concept.

Paul and Elder (2006) asserts that a strong critical thinker has such a broad spectrum of agility, versatility, and flexibility; flexibility in thought-critical reasoning, and how they are typically not easily tricked by slick argumentation, either by sophistry or intellectual trickery (p. 3). In addition, the fundamental and defining attribute of a strong-sense thinker is that he or she are both fair and just in their approach or relating to people, life, things, and circumstances. Or as in the case of "reflective assessment of the academic path of yesterday, up to and wholly including the current into the path of tomorrow; it ought to be approached in such a precise and systematic manner.

Next, the main purpose for engaging therein this ongoing activity is nothing less than the aversion of hindrances, distractions, or limitations, even if they are nothing more than cognitive or psychological in-nature. Having an open-mind, in fact, that is unbiased, and fair-minded to the past will afford an accurate understanding and hence the rightful extrapolation of pertinent information which can be fully utilized for many decades to come. In regards to the present academic-reality, I have decided to first and foremost monitor my own natural and innate propensity for egocentric thinking and thus actively engage therein the necessary or requisite actions, and then eliminate without hesitation or trepidation.

Nonetheless, the chief and primary purpose for this is to wholly ensure that a "team-first mindset" is not only promulgated, rather consistently preserved plus maintained at all times. Also, Paul and Elder (2006) affirms that "we can restrain our egocentrism only by developing explicit habits which enable us to do so" (p. 42). In other words, any form of self-driven and selfish thinking which ultimately hinders team connection and corroboration, as well as the development can be effectively removed if te individual first takes the initiative in placing it as a fundamental priority.

In brief, this ensures that nothing will hinder, thwart, or negatively affect one's contribution towards the applicable team, at the most elemental and individual-level. The necessary action for establishing a right relationship with my own mind; this is an action which requires self-accountability in my opinion, as well as personal responsibility.

Moreover, Paul and Elder (2006) avers "it should be clear that everyone lives in a special and intimate relationship to his or her own mindset" (p. 45). In other words, everyone literally possesses the special and innate capability for developing a relationship with their own mind; however, if the individual does not know this or has not been afforded the necessary tools, it will never become materialized. Only after this, in fact, relationship with self has been achieved, will the team be fully and thoroughly equipped for becoming in becoming fused together as one collective critical thinking unit. After all, critical thinking is as critical to the mind as high performance is to that of a sports car engine. Thus, over the course of both time and consistent repetition, critical thinking or high-performance thinking—regardless if at the individual or team-level, become nothing less than mere second-nature.

In a nutshell, now we do arrive at the substance of this particular discussion pertinent towards not only my personal theory-in-action, but also the relevant situational-circumstances involved.

Action-Activity, Circumstance, and Situation Formula

Identification and description of situation, 'S'. Regarding my current academic-situation, it is best described as one of the greatest anticipations, comprised of both invigoration and inquisitive-exploration. Hence, I am the least excited about having the opportunity for finally possessing a Ph.D. in Adult Education. Thus, the primary reason, as briefly discussed before, is at this precise point within the context of the collective doctoral-learning process, everything up to now has been but a series of crises, overflowing one into the next. In brief, it is best described as a continuum of misadventures, missed opportunities, adversity, and setbacks.

Hence, I would have preferred to have achieved my doctoral studies at least ten years ago. Unfortunately, as life so often occurs, rather than achieving this goal when I would have preferred, I instead found myself being abruptly and suddenly taken out of school in full plus active support of Operation Desert Shield, and Operation Desert Storm. This was a major setback that has literally taken twenty-two years to merely arrive at this critical academic-inflection *point-in-life*.

Identification and description of consequence, 'C'. Regarding my current consequence-reality, I have assertively decided to pursue my personal and professional goals with a relentless and unwavering state-of-mind. Hence, I have committed myself in approaching what otherwise might have discouraged any other. It is a circumstance that is nothing less than a priceless opportunity for long-lasting growth, positive change, and matured development. This can occur, in fact, by having a special relationship with my own inner system of advanced critical thinking and solution-finding. Paul and Elder (2006) corroborates that the mind is comprised of three rudimentary functional processes: 1. Thinking; 2. Feeling; and 3. Wanting. In other words, in order to maximize my continuum of past-to-current circumstances, I must first assess and critique as to whether or not what my authentic and true motivations are! This, in fact, is best interpreted as making sense f my reality-consequences.

Moreover, it requires accurate perception, open-minded analysis, and acute synthesis of retrieved evidence to fully support my list of assumptions. After thinking or reflecting thereon my objectives, and accurately distinguishing between wants, desires, and necessities, I can rightly assess my feeling-processes and the direct correlation that it has with the same set of objectives. Once these two functional processes, regarding the consequences of my reality has been actively engaged, will I be fully equipped in achieving my basic wants or academic-professional necessities. In brief, this step is comprised of understanding my goals, objectives, agendas, and deepest plus most intrinsic-motivations.

Chief Assumption Upon Which Author's Theory-in-Action Rests

An *assumption*, for starters, must not be confused with an *inference*. Thus, an "inference", or the act of inferring is to believe a thing to be accurate, even though in reality another thing is the true and accurate one. An "assumption", conversely, is a thing or idea that we often take-for-granted. We assume or presume that a thing or circumstance is to always exist as we believe. Paul and Elder (2006) defines an assumption as "something we take for granted or presuppose" (p. 73). This is the literal root from which the term "presupposition" is derived. Paul and Elder (2006) also aver that it is something we learned previously and do not challenge or question. It is a vital part of our belief system (p. 73).

Regarding challenging assumptions that currently comprises my current theory-in-action, they are categorized accordingly: 1. Humility; 2. Integrity; 3. Courage;

4. Interdependence of virtues. In other words, before anything else can occur, I must first approach with humility or the willingness to acknowledge any weakness which might hinder or impede one from having and arriving at a posture of "pure-understanding". To assume that everything I propose is accurate is ultimately a path-for-error and even inevitable failure in correct assumptions.

Hence, once a humble state-of-mind has been achieved, can I now clearly assess whether integrity exists at the core of my thought and understanding-foundation. If my integrity is lacking, ultimately the assumptions will be fragile, wavering, and unstable. Thus, my assumption must be established upon motives that are not self-centered or driven and influenced by nothing more than vainglorious and selfish propensities. And such, my accurate assumption can only be achieved by acting in the spirit of courage and relentless confidence in my own reasoning and systematic-mechanical thought-processes. Hence, the chief purpose is in the event of limitations or evidence or slightest error, I will be thoroughly equipped in pursuing the core objective until it has been achieved.

Lastly, there is the interdependence of intellectual virtues. All of the aforementioned virtues will be utilized not only individually, but also in a synergistic and harmonious-fashion.

In many instances, insofar, only a singular virtue may be active at one time. In other instances, conversely, there may be an interdependence of virtues that are required in order for the assumptions to be achieved, and the ultimate objective fully supported in direct correlation to my situation and circumstances.

Completion of the A→S = C

In my situation 'S', if I want to achieve consequence 'C', under assumptions $a(1) \ldots a(2) \ldots a(3) \ldots a(4) \ldots a(5) \ldots a(n)$, I will do or engage therein a certain activity 'A'. Hence, as it pertains to my current pursuit of doctoral studies 'S', if I desire to successfully matriculate towards attainment of Ph.D. 'C', under aforementioned assumptions, I must implement my current theory-in-action without trepidation.

In other words, I must commit to not only freeing myself from all forms or evidence of self-centered thinking, but also commit in establishing both a solid and sound relationship with my own system of thought and critical understanding, my own mind. In brief, only after these specific things have been utilized, will I be fully equipped in successfully achieving my ultimate life—personal, academic, and professional objective 'A'.

References

Argyris, C., & Schön, D. A. (1974). *Theory in practice: Increasing professional effectiveness*. (Reprinted ed.). San Francisco: Jossey-Bass.

Paul, R., & Elder, L. (2006). *Critical thinking: Tools for taking charge of your learning and your life*. (2nd ed.). Upper Saddle River, NJ: Pearson-Prentice Hall.

Supplemental Reading Material

Axelrod, A. (2010). Patton's Strange Genius. U.S. News and World Report: Secrets of America's Best Generals (Sp. ed.), 46.

Brands, H.W. (2011). Timing is Everything: 1862. Lincoln's Genius (Sp. Coll. ed.), 38.

Crabb, L. (1988). *Real change is possible-if you're willing to start from the inside out*. Colorado Springs, CO: NavPress.

Davis, D.A. (2010). The man with all the secrets. U.S. News and World Report: Secrets of America's Best Generals (Sp. ed.), 46.

James, M., & Jongeward, D. (1971). *Born to win: Transactional analysis with gestalt experiments*. Reading, MA: Addison-Wesley Publishing Company, Inc.

Swann, I. (1978). *Star fire: The shattering novel of the world's first psychic war.* New York, NY: Dell Publishing Co., Inc.

McKeachie, W.J., & Svinicki, M. (2006). *Teaching tips: Strategies, research and theory for college and university teachers*. New York, NY: Houghton Mifflin Company

Robbins, S.P. (2001). <u>Organizational Behavior</u>. (9th ed.). Upper Saddle River, NJ.

Swann, I. (1978). *Star fire: The shattering novel of the world's first psychic war.* New York, NY: Dell Publishing Co., Inc.

(1975). *Study guide to understanding psychology*. Del Mar, CA: Ziff-Davis Publishing Company

AUTHOR'S TRANSFORMING MINDSET

Hearts on Fire

The name of this section is *Hearts on Fire*. Proactively speaking; it must assertively be acknowledged, that the chief premise upon which the author has the drive and relentless perseverance plus tenacity to ensure that this comprehensive system is fully brought to fruition, is the song initially performed by the Beaver Brown Band. In fact, it was officially composed and performed by John Cafferty, as well as the Beaver brown Band; the origination date is 2006, and it can be found in the Rocky IV Movie Soundtrack.

In brief, the opening track is—Notice; Educational Purposes Only:

> Silent darkness creeps into your soul
> And removes the light of self-control
> The cave that holds you captive has no doors
> Burnin' with determination
> To even up the score.

Anyhow, the overarching idea is to think critically, identify, and thus submit, hence post "one word, song, or place that best describes", *who the author and students are, at the deepest and inner-most core*. Thus, in my honest opinion, the selected song cannot be limited to a one-dimensional context. In other words, even as in the case with many vast associates and colleagues who knows the author best, there exist no divide or compartmentalization regarding my collective and panoramic-life and existence. In brief, both the personal and professional quadrants of my rich life must be thus considered and approached in a collective or holistic frame-of-reference.

Next, the author deems it essentially necessary and vital to first submit a brief biographical sketch in direct response to the pair of questions; *who is Professor Shane Joseph Charbonnet? What it his background—personally and professionally?* For starters, the author currently resides with the Dallas/Ft. Worth Metroplex, Texas. He and his awesome wife have been married for twelve and one-half years. Professors Claude E. and Cedrina Patrice K. Bonet;

they both reside in the quiet and modestly-sized rural suburb, known as Cedar Hill. It is located about thirty-five minutes, geographically Southwest of Downtown Dallas. It is best recognized and described as a vibrantly eclectic, multi-cultural city of rich western historical significance and community-driven pride and distinction. As a side note, perhaps if time and happenstance affords, it will exist as a place listed at the top of your choice of preferred destinations.

Secondly, in regards to academic credentials, the author possesses a Bachelor of Science Degree in Computer Information Systems, with subsequent minors in Mathematics and Psychology. At the graduate-degree level, the author possesses a Master of Arts Degree in Professional Development. The core specialization is Leadership Studies and Management, plus Marketing.

Thirdly, the author is currently matriculating and hence successfully completing a Doctor of Philosophy Degree in Postsecondary and Adult Education. These additional courses and academic training is considered but vitally essential tools and instruments, all requisite in fulfilling a perpetual life of fulfillment—personally and professionally, as well as self-gratification.

Also, it will equip him to effectively contribute to the global society in a most promising and well-balanced manner. Thus, the aforementioned program will also equip the author in further developing such vital assets for overall and comprehensive life success, particularly within the context of greatly enhancing such vital assets in the following arena or discipline of Adult Education; it is an array of tools, such as:

- Critical thinking skills development;
- The mastery of self-understanding;
- Thinking outside-the-box;
- Writing effectively according to APA Standards;
- Increasing professional effectiveness;
- Becoming a competent-critical consumer;
- Effectiveness in team development and facilitation.

In brief, the anticipated end-result involves successfully completing the program, is that the participating student will become more equipped in effectively navigating and matriculating in the sphere of higher education, at both the graduate and post-graduate levels, while also holding part-time adjunct faculty positions as the local community college, as well as the local university campuses.

Moreover, as it pertains to the overall core subject at-hand, the chief or fundamental reason for selecting the aforementioned song—*Hearts on Fire*—is because I clearly illustrates the power of both relentless fervor, and uncompromising plus relentless passion, even in the face of overwhelming adversity, opposition, setbacks, intimidation, etcetera.

Hence, as the song clearly illustrates, there is a certain threshold that few individuals and students ever become qualified for crossing-over and there-into. This *cognitive-threshold*, as it were, involves literally at the core the full manifestation of a vociferous and all-consuming passion which disconnects and separates the participating individual from all feasibly alternative options. In fact, the only feasible option is to achieve the target goal or array of objectives set-before.

In a nutshell, it is this very same burning or *ever-consuming heart*, that distinguishes those who live and reside within a realm or dimension or great reward, limitless success, and complete plus total inner fulfillment, from those who live at the level of mediocrity and normalcy. Ultimately, it is this sheer passion that determines whether one achieves extraordinary success or self-deprecating failure. Choose wisely!

Thoughts, Re: Beyond-the-Stratosphere Thinking & Understanding

The initial challenge posed is to precisely identify a problem, issue, or challenge, and ultimately decide the *critical thinking path* which was selectively utilized in the initial identification process.

Foundational Premise

The first thing to actively consider is the idea or notion (cognitive-revelation) that this discussion will require such intentional thinking, that the typical utilization-levels of collective resources—mental, physical, and spiritual—may go beyond the norm. Moreover, *intentional thinking* is thinking which goes far above and beyond the meager path of the conventional thought process, status-quo. In other words, for any individual student learner to intentionally think, evaluate reason, assess, and make a definitive decision for action and determined implementation or facilitation.

This *stage of action*, hence, is followed by implementation, that will require the participating individual to assertively motivate him or herself in shifting paradigmatic ways of reasoning, thinking, and understanding and then transitioning from a passive stance to a more engaging and aggressive posture. In brief, it is such a posture which will ultimately result in perpetual change becoming fully and perhaps even irreversibly realized and materialized.

Recommended Strategy

The process requires the following steps to be actively and perpetually facilitated plus utilized. The specific steps include:

- Humility and liberation of thought;
- Self-transparency;
- Candid critical self-analysis and self-reflection or introspection;
- Engaging critique of one's critical thinking systematic processes;
- Willingness to negotiate with oneself first;
- Unhindered implementation of necessary or requisite steps for change.

Pragmatic Relevancy

The set time is now to awaken into a reality that if change was ever needed, it is indeed right now. One need not, in fact, go too too far in discovering and uncovering the vast gamut of issues, problems, and challenges that have literally infiltrated all levels of society. From the highest and most esteemed ivory towers of government, even to the lowest rank-and-file of blue collar America. Yes; there are unprecedented problems that must be rectified or else society as we know, will literally implode and become nothing more than a hapless capitulation.

In brief, these problems comprise the quandary of issues, challenges, and problems, and yet, in the author's candid and honest opinion, the only feasibly plus workable solution is the raising up and matriculation of a next-generation of high-level, fair-minded, as well as open-minded, and advanced critical thinkers, aka *Master of Hyper-meta Cognition*^{SM}.

The Colonel's Challenge

In regards to the initial question, as well as the initial challenge; it involves the dire need for attention—personally and professionally, in having a *Willingness for Engaging in Cognitive-Flexibility*. In other words, one must be willing to re-evaluate him or herself, inclusive of the application of personal theories in action, from a novel or fresh perspective, and thus engage therein the necessary systematic changes. Argyris and Schön (1974) assert "a theory in action" is nothing less than the integration of thought along with action.

Next, regarding the reason for identifying and implementing the necessary changes—from a holistic and long-term mindset, to eventually becoming a more able and efficient scholar, as well as more effective and well-rounded professional educator. An advance critical thinker whom is gifted and well qualified for effectuating change in the lives of the next-generation of both American and global sociocultural agents of change at-large.

The Set Path of Materialization and Success

Concerning the *actual path*, in which the author has utilized for arriving at this defining moment for fully realizing and achieving the collective goals and objectives, they are accordingly:

+ Humility;
+ Self-understanding;

⬇ Recognizing the interdependence of intellectual virtues (six stages of growth and development);

⬇ Identify the actual stage in which one exists;

⬇ Utilize courage to change, integrity for honesty with self, and perseverance for following through literally until the end.

In other words, only after acquiescing unto a state of humbleness of heart and mind, will I be fully equipped for affording myself both sound and balanced critical feedback. Thus, the recommendation for self-correction will be free of either subjectivity-biased thinking, as well as fickle emotionalism.

Secondly, as a direct result of having the right *frame of thought*, will one guard him or herself from being influenced by subjective or otherwise ego-centric driven thinking. The decision-making process will not be negatively influenced by an erroneous or superficial approach that would otherwise hinder growth, and development from taking place.

Thirdly, before progressing any further on the maturity-continuum, one must have the sound understanding that the objective will only be achieved by actively utilizing a combination of requisite intellectual virtues.

Next, the actual stage that the author currently exists on the critical thinking mountain-pyramid, must be identified and thoroughly assesses plus analyzed. Hence, the main purpose for this step is to not only understand *where one originates from*, as well as *where one currently resides*, if you prefer, rather on the contrary equipping oneself in the full development of the necessary and requisite strategies for eventually arriving at and hence achieving the ultimate objective.

This ultimate objective is the highest-level of growth and cognitive-development. Only after all of the aforementioned dynamics have been effectively utilized, will one be in the right posture or cognitive frame-of-reference for experiencing long-lasting critical thinking growth and development; also change and holistic quantum maturation. The actual stage of development, moreover, in which the author firmly believes that he currently exists, is stage three (3).

In short, stage three is identified or defined as the "beginning thinker stage". Paul and Elder (2006) affirm that a thinker whom is a beginning or elementary-level thinker, he or she possesses the following array of distinctive attributes:

- Analyzes the logic of situations and problems;
- Expresses clear and precise questions;
- Checks information for accuracy and relevancy;
- Distinguishes between raw information and someone's interpretation of it;
- Recognizes assumptions guiding inferences;
- Identifies prejudicial and biased beliefs, unjustifiable conclusions, misused words, and missed implication;
- Notices when our viewpoint is biased by one's selfish or narcissistic interests.

References

Argyris, C., & Schön, D.A. (1974). *Theory in practice.* San Francisco, CA: Jossey-Bass Publishers.

Paul, R., & Elder, L. (2006). *Critical thinking tools for taking charge of your learning and your life.* (2nd ed.). New Jersey: Prentice Hall.

Elements of Perception Model

The purpose for this novel approach to higher education is to not only address or respond to the vastly dynamic challenges in a linear or *one-dimensional context*, rather most importantly, for the sake of rightly applying and effectively utilizing some of the tools and resources recommended for a strong-sense and fair-minded critical thinker. In fact, Paul and Elder (2006) divulge that a "fair-minded thinker" is such a quality of individual who when it comes to engaging therein and thus making decisions, strongly considers the need, interests, concerns, opinions, and desires of others, rather than one's own selfish desires, needs, wants, predilections ambitions, goals, and desires (p. 1).

The learner is most interested, moreover, in not simply learning the content, hence digesting the listed tools, strategies, and techniques, but most importantly applying and utilizing in an acutely relevant *360-degree critical thinking context*. Also, the author has opted to respond to the set discussion parameters by utilizing a few strategies or techniques discussed here.

In direct response to the question; *what is the elements of thought model.* Paul and Elder (2006) asserts that the elements of thought can also be referred to as vital parts or compartments of critical thinking; the fundamental structures of thought (p. 55).

In other words, anytime an individual engages therein critical thinking at any level, there are fundamental parts of elements of reasoning that plays a vital role in the process of arriving at the desired conclusions thereof. The *elements of thought* are categorized into eight distinctly rudimentary quadrants, as follows:

- Fundamental purpose;
- Key question being answered;
- Information considered as vital necessity;
- The most basic concept;
- Assumptions being utilized;
- Point-of-view;
- Fundamental inferences or conclusions;
- Implications of reasoning process (p. 58).

Selected Article Relevant to Theme

Adult Learning; it is a concept that has literally exploded in relevancy and popularity within just the last few years. At the fundamental core, it involves individuals, many whom have either merely started or even matriculated from a learning institution many years prior to; it includes single mothers, fathers, or even working adults, all whom have arrived at the decision to go back to school and either finish their academic studies or simply achieving higher degrees of learning.

Moreover, as in the specific case of many colleagues of the author, there is a vastly and almost expeditious migration back into learning circles—traditionally and 21st Century. And yet, what would adult education be without the development of relevant or pertinent theories, modalities, concepts, or principles. In brief, the main purpose is to briefly assess and evaluate an article and actively discuss or critique a few questions through the active utilization of Richard Paul and Linda Elder's *Elements of Thought Theoretical Model*.

The name of this overarching discussion is "Andragogy and Self-directed Learning: Pillars of Adult Learning Theory". The corresponding author is Professor Sharan B. Merriam of the University of Georgia at Athens. Regarding the presumed purpose of the article's fundamental premise; the author firmly believes that it involves the direct correlation between adult learners as well as the array of methods, strategies, tools, patterns, and techniques often involved in the applicable path of learning. This presupposition is reinforced in the opening sentence; Professor Merriam (2001) avers "the central question of how adults learn has occupied the attention of scholars and practitioners since the founding of adult education as a professional field of practice in the 1920s" (p. 1).

In brief, the article delves not only into the fundamentals of structural schematics of adult learning as a formulation of mere or meager processes, rather as a requisite series of core pillars that are most essential in order for the comprehensive education of adults to become fully materialized and realized.

Strategic-Tactical Approach

It is noted that the article has been fragmented or sub-divided into seven (7) basic or rudimentary components.

The *first component* (paragraph one) is entitled "Early Research in Adult Learning". Included within, in fact, the author actively investigates and researches into the historical components and relevancy of adult learning, not only as a mere or meager theoretical learning concept, but *how it is pragmatically applied into the context of higher academic learning structures or systems*. Hence, this involves a direct reference to a book utilized in her research entitled, "Adult Learning" (Thorndike, Bregman, Tilton, and Woodyard).

In brief, it is a book that was published two years succeeding the formulation or adult education as a widely-revered and respected academic system. He author submits, "Thorndike and others approached adult learning from a behavioral psychological perspective" (p. 3).

The *second component* (paragraph two) is entitled "Andragogy". It is a concept of adult education; it was first developed by Malcolm Knowles (1968). It is distinguished from pre-adult schooling, as well as other systems of learning, by the context of both labels and relevant technology. It is a direct contrast to pedagogy or the "art and science of teaching youth"—children education (Merriam, 2001, p. 5). It is defined by Knowles as a matter-of-fact as "the art and science of aiding and helping adult-level students maximize learning (Merriam, 2001, p. 5).

In brief, regarding the purpose for this innovative approach, it's ultimate objective, hence relative purpose is to distinguish adult education from other forms of education, inclusive of pre-school, elementary, intermediate, middle, and high school.

The *third component* (paragraph three) is entitled or categorized as "Science, and Technology". This involves the ongoing investigation into the possibility of adult education being wholly considered and recognized as a scientific study, academic discipline, and it's connection thereof with computer technology-electronics. Hence, adult education is considered from the vantage point of electronics, hardware, products, computers, theories, modalities, academic study, applications and research.

In brief, it is approached as a movement for becoming firmly established as a legitimate scientific discipline. Thus, rather than approaching and considering effective education as either a science, academic discipline, or mere technological studies, hence applications, the author proposes that in order for effective and matured adult education to take place, all of the vital elements must be actively considered as one-collective until, as opposed to individually.

Hence, the remaining elements or components include:

- Context-free Andragogy;
- Self-directed learning;
- The goals;

- The processes;
- The Learner;
- Current assessment of SDL.

Encompassing Question

The main question is; *what evidence, if any, does the author provide to indicate that his or her assumptions are based on an organized theory?*

Before progressing any further, it must be noted that step five (5) will be utilized! It has been directly extrapolated directly from 'Exhibit 4.2 Diagram'; it involves the "Universal Structures of Thought". Hence, step five is described by Paul and Elder as the "utilization of data, facts, and experiences" (2006, p. 56). In other words, this process involves the application of identified or retrieved factual evidence which but only further reinforces the author's central assumption. The result will exist as *true* or *false*; *applicable* or *non*-applicable; *relevant* or irrelevant; lastly, it also will exist as *supported* or *failed-to-support*.

Secondly; as it relates to the author's direct correlation to an "organized theory", it appears that the fundamental assumption is for organized theory to be utilized, "Andragogy and self-directed learning continues to be important and significant to our present-day understanding of adult learning". In other words, even though adult learning has progressively evolved over the course of the past decades, there clearly exist a relevancy between the art and science of adult learning, and self-directed adult learning. In brief, both concepts of *Andragogy* and *Self-directed learning* exist as fundamental pillars of the facilitation of the comprehensive adult learning process.

Next, pertinent to the evidence utilized by Professor Merriam to support her thesis or core assumption, they are accordingly:

- Identification of five assumptions which underlies the concept of Andragogy;
- Reference to the work of a few pioneers in the field of adult education.

Thirdly, in regards to the specific reference to the *Andragogy discussion*, Professor Merriam (2001) states that "the five assumptions underlying Andragogy describe the adult learner as someone who:

- Has an independent self-concept and can direct his or her own learning;
- Has accumulated a reservoir of life experiences that is a rich resource for learning;
- Has learning needs closely related to changing social roles;
- Is problem-centered and interested in immediate application of knowledge;
- Is motivated to learn by internal, rather than external factors (p. 5).

In brief, the assumptions proposed by Malcolm Knowles are that there exist a direct connection and relevance between the overall concept of Andragogy and comprehensive adult learning. Hence, not only is Andragogy a concept with sound factual supporting evidence, it is also a critical and vital component of effectively establishing new and novel methods of adult-level learning.

As it, in fact, correlates to Knowles's innovative concept, and he chief premise held by Merriam, adults are—due to their mature and independent-nature—capable in matriculating through their individual academic-learning process with little, if no support or assistance at all. In brief, this is successfully achieved even though many instructors play some role in the overall structure of the adult-learning system-experience.

Next, as it relates to the specific evidence supporting the discussion, Professor Merriam makes direct reference to several revered pioneers in the field of adult education. The *pioneers*, in fact, which are mentioned, thus includes:

- Houle;
- Tough;
- Knowles.

As a direct result of the ground-breaking work of these aforementioned individuals; "early research in self-directed learning was descriptive, verifying the widespread presence of self-directed learning amongst adults and documenting the process by which it occurred"

(2001, p. 8). The innovators only confirmed and proved that self-directed learning was prevalent, but also most effective in the overall training and development of adults whom had aspired unto a higher dimension of learning, and in most cases improved the overall quality-of-living.

In brief, not only was SDL considered relevant back then, it has become so popular that in our contemporary or neo-modern era, that it might well become the future of adult education. Thus Merriam goes a few steps further in boldly declaring that "clearly, there are numerous possibilities for how future research on self-directed learning might enrich the lives of adult learners, as well as greatly contribute to the theory of adult education as a germane and potent theoretical learning framework.

In closing, Professor Merriam is wholly convinced that there exist no individual theory, model, sets of principles, explanations or concepts that acutely explain how adult learning in academic environments is effective. Thus, in order to explain and understand the comprehensive realm of adult education, a mosaic of theories, models, and sets of principles, explanations or concepts must be considered, without haste.

Regarding the context of this article, there are two fundamental concepts that are considered of most importance; the concepts of *Andragogy*, and *Self-directed Learning*. In other words, the author is convinced that these fundamental pillars of adult learning will continue to increase in not only relevancy, but also the development and facilitation of the comprehensive learning process. Merriam (2001) concludes that "a more likely scenario is that both of these pillars of adult learning theory will continue to engender debate, discussion, and research, and in so doing, further contribute and enrich or understanding of adult learning" (p. 11).

Disclaimer Notice: the article was retrieved from the Specialization Resource Collection (SRC)) Website. It is located and extrapolated from the web-link: http://www.media.capella.edu/CourseMedia/ed8002/minisite/pae_library.aspx

Reference

Merriam, S.B. (2001). Andragogy and self-directed learning [Electronic version]. Pillars of Adult Learning Theory, 89, 3-13.

Paul, R., & Elder, L. (2006). *Critical thinking: Tools for taking charge of your learning and your life*. (2ⁿᵈ ed.). Upper Saddle River, NJ: Pearson-Prentice Hall.

MOTIVATIONAL THEORIES (3) & IMPACT UPON CONTEMPORARY CONCEPTS

Abstract

For starters, the motivational which exist as the main pillars of this section were all created, developed, and facilitated during the 1950s. Each one, individually and collectively, profess that human beings are greatly influenced by a series of factors which occur within the context of his or her environment. These stimulating forces, in fact, can either be of a positive or negative derivation. In brief, they can also exist intrinsically and extrinsically, or mutually at-the-same-time.

According to *Abraham Maslow's Hierarchy of Needs Model*, human needs are categorized or classified into two very distinct levels; the first (one) being the lower-level aka *negative factors*, or conversely the higher-level aka *positive factors*. The other theories, which are not as commonplace as the hierarchy of needs, includes: 1. Theory 'X'; 2. Theory 'Y'. Yet, unlike Maslow's Theory, Theory 'X' and Theory 'Y'—both developed and proposed by Douglas McGregor, focuses on the proposition that there does exist two distinct viewpoints pertinent to the human existence, as well as their behavioral-motivational patterns, hence *motivational predilections*.

In other words, there exist a list of factors which are either of a negative or positive origin, and the source of that origination in having a significant impact upon the actions of human beings. Nonetheless, it is from the establishment of the foundational theories, upon which a very large and significant majority of contemporary theoretical frameworks have originated. Thus, the ultimate purpose of this thesis is to provide some profound, richly keen insights, into the core intricacies of each and every one of the three foundational theories, and *how they are significantly differentiated one from the other*; all through the utilization of a brief list sources which expounds upon each individual topic, as abstracted from the corresponding E-textbook.

Concepts upon Which Contemporary Theories Are Established

The underlying question is; *what is it that drives individuals to do certain things, or even act in a pattern of behavior whether rational or irrational*? After all, for all action(s) ought not to be considered as direct result of some specific activity or series of actions, which preceded that same result. Regardless of: 1. Age; 2. Gender; 3. Race; 4. Religion; 5. Cultural background; 6. Ethnicity, all actions are caused by some *stimulating force*—externally or internally in source.

Next, this phenomenon, commonly referred to as motivating factors, has perplexed the hearts and minds of countless millions-to-tens of millions of diverse individuals; dating even as far back as the dawning of the earliest civilizations of mankind. For example, some individuals prefer a certain flavor of drink, whereas another person possesses a rather biased preference in regards to the certain style of outer garb which he or she opts and thus chooses to be attired. Hence, another individual might even demonstrate a distinct habitual pattern in the way he or she actively responds to specific stimuli.

Nonetheless, Contemporary Theorists conclude that people are directly influenced, wither positively or negatively, based upon the fulfillment of certain generalized human needs; needs in fact that are very real, and profoundly significantly impact and influence the actions of individuals—collectively and individually. These needs as expressed by motivational theorists are defined as: 1. Need for personal achievement and fulfillment; 2. Need for personal power; 3. Need for justice and mutual fairness; 4. Need for reward or compensation for personal sacrifice, as well as efficient performance.

In other words, these modern day and contemporary concepts are actually established upon the concepts developed many years prior to, be several nameless human behavioral theorists. Although there were four foundational theories, which were established and developed during the 1950s, for the sake of time-management and avoiding the limitless list of possible complexities, the content of this report will focus upon only three. These specific theories were crafted, developed, and engineered, by their *founding fathers*;

Abraham Maslow and Douglas McGregor, both of whom the concepts forever changed the face of the *full insightful understanding of human behavior*, here again as they directly correlates towards external and internal stimuli.

Hierarchy of Human Needs Model; Abraham Maslow

It was first developed and thus proposed by its founding father, Abraham Maslow. It is actually firmly established upon another common and popular theory, as defined by Stephen Robbins; it asserts that every human being's actions are directly connected to the five basic needs which are a necessity towards the attainment of satisfaction being fully achieved and realized. Professor Maslow reveals that the need for self-actualization proposes that individuals are driven by internal influencers, which have a direct impact upon the human psyche.

That is, literally all human beings, in general, possess an internal plus innate need for performing at his or her optimum-level, and of course the total actualization of the utter fulfillment of goals, and personal dreams becoming manifested. However, if those same needs are not met, resulting disastrous performance is expected to be greatly reduced.

Next, at the direct opposite of the human-needs continuum, the need for physiological fulfillment also has a direct impact. The needs for physical fulfillment are sub-divided according to the basic human need for survival, such as: 1. Hunger; 2. Thirst; 3. Shelter; 4. Sexual fulfillment; 5. Bodily functional propensities. In brief, these needs are considered as being both external and extrinsic contributing factors, which consequentially if not met, usually poses a significant impact upon the individual's decisions, actions, and even resulting behavioral patterns.

Moreover, pertinent to the hierarchy itself, the chief and primary reason for Maslow's listing of the human needs in a hierarchical or *pyramid-shaped schematics layout*, is because Maslow personally considered the achievement of human needs as a logical process.

In order for the higher-level or intrinsic needs to have the slightest possibility for being realized, thus fulfilled, it is vitally imperative that the lower-level needs first be addressed plus met. Unlike Maslow, in which his list of needs focuses more upon the logical flow of fulfillment, Douglas McGregor's Theory 'X' is established upon the following for pillars.

The *first pillar*; employees inherently dislike work, and whenever possible will attempt to avoid it.

The *second pillar*; considering that employees really dislike having to work, must be forced or coerced, controlled, or threatened, in order to achieve very desirable results.

The *third pillar*; whenever possible, employees will shirk responsibility, as well as seeking out formal directives. The *fourth and final pillar*; employees will place the need for security far above all other factors.

Theory 'Y'; conversely, it is a direct contrast o that of Theory 'X', by the sheer fact that employee motivation is stimulated from a more positive perspective. That is, there is greater focus upon the rewards, and the incentives of those employed. And such, the key defining factor which significantly differentiates Theory 'X' from Theory 'Y' is based upon *psychological perspectives*. For example, within the context of Theory 'X', work is viewed as an inconvenience, as opposed to a priceless opportunity for being active or participative in a positive (+) way.

Also, another very significant difference between the two opposing theories is that under Theory 'X', people must be coerced, controlled, and basically intimidated into performing diverse tasks, whereas under the overarching umbrella of Theory 'Y', people are committed towards taking the actions in the demonstration of self-directed, self-management techniques.

In other words, in retrospect back towards Maslow's Theory for human motivation, Theory 'X' assumes that lower-level needs are the dominating plus stimulating factors in regards to human behavior and motivation. In brief, Theory 'X' assumes that lower-level needs are the dominating force in regards to human motivation, whereas Theory 'Y, conversely, assumes that the need for utter fulfillment of higher-order needs is the most significant, hence driving motivating factor.

Application of Theories to Workplace Environment

On a much more personal note; pertinent to Professor Abraham Maslow's Theory of Hierarchical Human Needs, I have experienced a situation in which there existed the hyper-abundance of work demands, and the lack thereof of suitable employees to accomplish or perform those specific duties. Hence, as it relates to the priorities set by those individuals, it is both apparent and evident that the primary motivating factors, applicable to the management of their time, as well as the performance of the specific duties, the *Need for Personal Esteem*, literally exists at the top of the list.

Next, the attitude of a particular and nameless employee—germane to their responsibilities was, *I am not going to do anything or accept any amount of responsibilities which would either belittle or minimize my most **esteemed-level of expertise**, as a respected and revered professional.* Thus, rest assured, the need for feeling good about one, and the level of respect as demonstrated in the eyes of his or her encompassing colleagues and peers, was apparently considered of the greatest importance.

Thirdly, regarding Theory 'Y'; I can also recollect a time while working at the aforementioned corporation, that a large portion of the support staff were consistently filing complaints that there was too much demands and burdensome pressures placed upon them by the staff of management. Apparently the managers who were chiefly responsible for the facilitation of assignments and tasks were not affording the employee with the freedom, flexibility, and liberty for utilizing his or her creative plus innovation abilities and demonstrating acts of independence and self-direction.

In brief, the result and productivity of the organization, as any reasonable individual cannot even begin to fathom, was grossly despicable and horrible.

Chief Method or Cornerstone

The detailed information utilized in dissecting each foundational method was acquiesced through very careful comparative analytics—compare and contrast, of pertinent information provided in the E-textbook, as utilized throughout the overall breadth, depth, and length of this brief yet most comprehensive thesis. As carefully discussed plus listed by the corresponding E-textbook author, Professor Stephen Robbins; information was heretofore abstracted and extrapolated from the same text, in order to define and bring unhindered illumination to the material of the text, as related to the overarching concept of human motivational theory.

Human Motivation Theories/Formal Conclusion

As one reflects and thoughtfully considers modern day human behavior, and how it directly is impacted and influenced by external plus internal motivational factors, it is vitally important that the same individual direst carefully dissect and then be able to fully extrapolate the theories as proposed by Maslow and McGregor. Otherwise, if that same individual would be so naïve and blinded to not consider the information proposed by each of the proven theorists, the list of factors which could possibly affect the core essence of the decision-making process, particular activities performed, and certain behavioral patterns that would otherwise be complex plus overwhelming and most time-consuming.

Hence, not only has each theorist provided a *narrowed-list* which incorporates all of the limitless vast possibilities, but also defined and clarifies certain issues in such a manner which can very easily be thoroughly comprehended and understood. Understood even by the most untrained and unlearned, ordinary individuals.

Reference

Robbins, S.P. (2001). *Organizational behavior*. (9th ed.). Upper Saddle River, NJ.

GENESIS OF THE |QUÅNTUM| ACAD(YNA^{E3})MICS ACADIO-SPHERE

Abstract

Appreciative Inquiry (AI); it is a critical aspect pertinent to the development and growth of all organizations. It is considered, within the field of organizational development, as a most important plus vital component necessary for long-lasting comprehensive success. It is comprised, in fact, of nothing less than the meager gesture of asking questions. Preskill and Catsambas (2006) assert that in order for "organizations and communities to move forward, to reach their goals in an unpredictable world, it is critical that we begin to ask more questions" (p. 1). Also, regarding this project's chief objective, it involves the comprehensive assessment-evaluation of a hypothetical situation. In other words, it will be achieved by designing an evaluation plan, creation of relevant and necessary information, and lastly the drafting of an executive summary. In brief, this project is comprised of the following sections:

1. Introduction;
2. Evaluation Plan;
3. Interview Protocol;
4. Draft Instrumentation;
5. Executive Summary;
6. Final Appreciative Inquiry Evaluation Plan.

Chief Premise

"No one ever attains very eminent success by simply doing what is required of him; it is the amount of excellence of what is over and above the required that determines the greatness of ultimate distinction" (McLellan quoting Adams, C.K., 1998, p. 87).

Section One: Introduction

AI is defined by Preskill and Catsambas (2006) as "a group process that inquires into, identifies, and further develops the best of 'what is' in organizations in order to create a better future" (p. 1). It is a process, in fact, fundamentally ascribed as the act of an organization engaging into an ongoing series of critical questioning. AI fundamentally involves nothing less than a necessary process for which an ongoing and long-lasting metamorphosis, involving progressive change, inevitably results.

Insofar, it is utilized and implemented with the underlying intent of developing an organization that is not only viable and relevant, rather most importantly effective in effectuating comprehensive change within the context of its local, regional, and perhaps even global spheres of influence. Thus, before this objective can be achieved; however, a hypothetical situation will first be constructed and critically considered. In other words, do we arrive at the key theme of this first section of the AI Evaluation Plan Project; the name of this section is the "Introduction Section". In brief, it is thus comprised thereof the following core components:

1. Explanation of the hypothetical situation, including the vision, mission, values, and goals of the organization;
2. Purpose of the evaluation;
3. Statement regarding the applicability of AI to the evaluation effort and situation.

Explanation of the Hypothetical Situation

In regards to the first element—*hypothetical situation*, it involves an organization that was initially designed and facilitated with the underlying intent of effectuating long-lasting constructive change within the framework of its corresponding spheres of influence. Hence, *The |Quantum| Acad(yna*^{E3}*)mics* Academy; it serves to afford every one of its corresponding learners-partners both the necessary educational tools plus resources, all required for successfully matriculating through the overall breadth and length of the program. It also affords a resolute and unwavering foundation upon which long-lasting success will ultimately become a reality.

In other words, the *main problem at*-hand, which initially predicated the drafting and utilization of the AI, involving addressing, dealing with, and ultimately resolving the diverse issues which will but only hinder the aforementioned partners from fully realizing their academic, as well as vocational goals and objectives. In brief, it is safe to say that the overall chief vision of the organization is to become nothing less than a beacon of direction, guidance, and hope for not only its partners-affiliates, rather most importantly the all encompassing world at-large.

Concerning the *overall mission*, secondly, of the organization, it is constructed upon the notion of affording diverse solutions pertinent directly to the vastly unfathomable problems pervading and thus permeating the world in which one resides. In brief, a succinct list of specific services that the |Quåntum| Acad(yna^{E3})mics Academy affords include:

1. Provision of critical tools and resources, such as media, books, pamphlets, network and relevant affiliates;
2. A sound and unwavering academic foundation relevant to the field of interest;
3. A variety of effective strategies and techniques which can be used on an individual-basis.

Concerning both the *values and goals*, thirdly, of the |Quåntum| Acad(yna^{E3})mics Academy, they are literally one-in-the-same. In other words, the values and goals (main agenda) of this cutting-edge and innovative academy-entity is best summarized in stating that it places greater emphasis upon the change, development, and the overall growth of its partners as being of the utmost priority, second to none. In brief, the organization's main agenda involves:

1. Provision of an optimal-level learning environment;
2. Construction of bridges between instructors, learners, and prospective recipients of leadership, and effective counsel;
3. Development of leaders whom are balanced, competent, and unapologetically empathetic—in a horizontal as well as vertical context.

Next, pertinent to the customers to whom the organization specifically targets, it fundamentally comprises students, practicing educators of facilitators of education, plus knowledge, and the encompassing communities at-large.

Finally, pertinent to affording a response to the question; *what is the community context in which the overall program will be facilitated*. The answer is simply; it is triple-tiered. The *first-tier* involves the local community, specifically located in the institution's chief locale, Dallas/ Ft. Worth Metroplex. The group to whom the services will be afforded includes anyone interested in being taught and trained, concerning the underlying discussion of holistic human development and human performance. The *second-tier* involves the regional community. This includes all individuals residing within one hundred square mile proximity. The *third and final tier* involves the vastly diverse individuals or prospective learners whom reside beyond or outside of the one-hundred mile proximity, inclusive of those whom even reside in a foreign country. In brief, concerning the specific services in which the program will afford, it also focuses thereon maximized holistic human development, as well as human performance.

Purpose and Target of Evaluation Correlating to Hypothetical Problem

Regarding the *second element*—clarifying the purpose and target of the evaluation, the underlying purpose and target actually exist under a singular and overshadowing umbrella, called "holistic proactive and comprehensive effectiveness". The evaluation serves to, henceforth, address, identify, and respond to the weaknesses or deficiencies of the overall, yet wholly encompassing academic system. It also conversely affords working solutions requisite for eventually developing a working strategic system which results in learners whom are balanced, competent, and highly effective.

Thus, it is a novel and innovative strategic method that essentially affords what is currently considered as the most effective, as well as expedient solution(s) necessary for addressing and responding to the prevalent issues, plus challenging the very fabric of our society. In brief, the chief purpose for even engaging therein the particulars of the evaluation process s fundamentally established upon the idea and notion that:

1. There are vastly threatening issues which if not dealt with, will hinder and impede the overall success of the organization—short-term and long-term;
2. The very life and underlying vitality of the organization rests upon its ability to proactively address, hence fully eradicate the challenges, issues, and problems which wither does exist or even has yet to exist.

Concerning the *overall target*, moreover, of the evaluation plan; it involves nothing less than the total eradication and thus obliteration of all challenges, issues, and problems that directly hinders and otherwise threatens—present and future context—short-term and long-term success of the organization. Next, as it pertains to the chief cornerstone of the |Quåntum| Acad(yna^{E3})mics^{SM} Acadio-sphere, the comprehensive purpose and target of the AI Evaluation Plan involves the perpetual and progressive change, development, and growth of an organization. One in fact that is equipped in not only dealing with diverse issues, and the creation of an organization that is successful is effectuating positive change applicable to one corresponding spheres of influence. In brief, this can only be achieved by the key leaders of the organization affording each and every one of its corresponding learners and partners the necessary educational instrument, resources, and tools.

Description of the AI and Applicability to Evaluation Effort

Regarding the *third and final element*—affording both a description of the AI, and applicability towards the evaluation effort. For starters, it is established upon the idea that the first essential act engage therein, involves the generation as well as the facilitation of as many questions of reflection and critical inquiry as possible. Hence, the first stage of the AI involves the corresponding group participants inquiring therein; to also identify, and develop the most comprehensive list of infinite possibilities, regardless of how absurd, foolish, or ridiculous they might initially be considered as. It is a most thorough and fully comprehensive process, defined by Preskill and Catsambas (2006) as "a group process that inquires into, identifies, and further develops the best 'what if' in organization, in order to create a better and brighter future" (p. 1). A brief list of feasible question which perhaps will arise, they include:

1. What is the current status of the organization;
2. What current challenges, issues, and problems threaten the overall success of the organization;
3. What solutions—procedures, strategies, techniques ought to be created that directly addresses and responds to the list of dynamic challenges, issues, and problems;
4. How will the organization prepare itself for future unforeseen situations, as well as unanticipated plus unforeseen crises;

5. What takeaways or *nuggets of wisdom* have been collected, and thoroughly processed for immediate future reference.

Lastly, in regards to a working AI Model that is considered both pertinent and relevant to the overall AI Evaluation Plan, it is formally known as the *4-D Model*. The 4-D Model, which was first developed by David Cooperrider while completing his doctoral studies at Case Western University (1980); it consists of four phases:

1. Discovery Phase;
2. Dream Phase;
3. Design Phase;
4. Destiny Phase (Preskill and Catsambas noting Cooperrider et al., 2003; 2006, p. 15).

4-D Model

The *Discovery Phase*; it involves the notion of the individual, or corresponding list of participants, both identifying and classifying the relevant particulars of the overall evaluation plan itself, as it correlates to the organization and its overall longevity of success.

The *Dream Phase*; it addresses the idea of corresponding team players engaging into the comprehensive process of utilizing their vast plus dynamic assortment of creative, imaginative, and innovative-innate abilities or skills. The underlying purpose is to design a quasi-dimensional plan that is capable and most flexible in responding to any situation, regardless if anticipated or even unforeseen.

The *Design Phase*; it involves nothing less than the actual moment when transition occurs between innovation and application, hence execution. In brief, this is the actual moment when all of the activity which occurred in steps one and two actually becomes to officially get set-in-motion.

The *Destiny Phase*; it is the actual moment when much needed results begin to materialize. In brief, this is the key defining phase when all of the labor and investment which occurred prior to, begins to finally show evidence of life, productivity, ad overall comprehensive vitality.

Next, the Appreciative Inquiry (AI) is fundamentally established upon the following core question, "what is wrong with the human side of the organization" (Preskill, and Catsambas, 2006, p. 9). Hence, it is the chief pillar upon which all of the other elements or tenets of the comprehensive AI is constructed and rests thereon. While Dr. Cooperrider, in fact, was pursuing his postgraduate studies, he swiftly began to notice the direct affect that the facilitation of questions made upon the overall morale or motivation of the relevant team members or the organization. Dr. Cooperrider, insofar, noticed that "when he asked questions that were problem-focused, people lost energy and became less engaged with the interview" (Preskill, and Catsambas, 2006, p. 9).

In closing, when the same organization and her participants were questioned regarding "why things succeeded, the interviewees' level of interest and energy increased" (Preskill, and Catsambas, 2006, p. 9). In brief, the overall success of the |Quåntum| Acad(yna^{E3})mics Academy rests thereon the ability of its key players being able to effectively facilitate the 'right question'; an effective facilitation in such a way that constructive productivity both results and perpetually continues for multiplied decades to come.

Conclusion

AI is considered as a critical aspect of the overall development and growth of all organizations. It asserts that organizational success cannot be achieved unless it first decides to commit towards constructing a firm and unwavering foundation. AI is also defined, in fact, by Professors Preskill and Catsambas (2006) as "a group process that inquires into, identifies, and further develops the best of 'what is' in organizations, in order to create a better future" (p. 1). It fundamentally involves nothing less than a necessary process for which a long-lasting and ongoing metamorphosis or progressive change results in the end. AI is comprised of the following core components:

1. Explanation of the hypothetical situation, including the vision, mission, values, and goals of the organization;
2. Purpose of the evaluation;
3. Statement regarding the applicability of AI to the evaluation effort and situation.

Regarding the hypothetical situation, it involves an organization that was initially designed and facilitated with the underlying intent of effectuating long-lasting plus constructive change within the framework of its corresponding spheres of influence. In brief, the organization's main agenda involves:

1. Provision of an optimal-level learning environment;
2. Construction of bridges between instructors, learners, and prospective recipients of leadership, and effective counsel;
3. Development of leaders whom are balanced, competent, and unapologetically empathetic.

Regarding the clarification of the chief purpose, as well as target of the evaluation, it actually exists under a singular and overshadowing umbrella—*holistic proactive and comprehensive effectiveness*. In other words, as it relates back to the |Quåntum| Acad(yna^E3)mics Acadio-sphere, the comprehensive purpose and target of the AI Evaluation Plan involves the perpetual and progressive change, development, and growth of an organization that is wholly equipped in not only dealing with diverse issues, rather most importantly the creation and engineering of such an organization that is most successful in effectuating constructive, plus positive change with the context of the learners sphere of influence—locally, regionally, and globally.

Regarding affording both a description of the AI, and its applicability towards the evaluation effort, it is established upon the idea or notion that the first act to engage therein involves the generation of as many *questions of inquiry and reflection, and critical inquiry*, as feasibly possibly.

Lastly, regarding the working of the AI Model, it is formally known as the *4-D Model*. The 4-D Model is comprised of the following four core phases:

Phase of discovery;

1. Phase of dreaming;
2. Phase of designing;
3. Phase of destiny-realization.

The first phase fundamentally involves the notion of the individual or corresponding participators both identifying, and classifying the relevant particulars of the overall evaluation plan itself, particularly as it relates to the organization, and its overall longevity of success.

The second phase addresses the idea of team players engaging into the comprehensive process of utilizing their creative and innovative-innate abilities plus skills. The third phase involves nothing less than the actual moment when transitioning takes place between innovation realization, and application-execution. The fourth and final phase can best be summarized with affirming that this is the actual moment when lasting results begin to realize. In closing, the AI is established upon the following underlying question; "what is wrong with the human side of the organization" (Preskill, and Catsambas, 2006, p. 9). In brief, the overall success of the |Quåntum| Acad(yna^{E3})mics Acadio-sphere rests upon the ability of its key players being able to facilitate the array of questions and answers in such a way that productivity both results and perpetually exists for multiplied decades to come.

References

McLellan, V. (1998). *Wise words and quotes: An intriguing collection of popular quotes by famous people and wise sayings from scripture.* Wheaton, IL: Tyndale House Publishers, Inc.

Preskill, H., & Catsambas, T.T. (2006). *Reframing evaluation through appreciative inquiry.* Thousand Oaks, CA: Sage Publications.

Section Two: Evaluation Plan (EPS)

The EPS is comprised of the following core, yet fundamental components:

1. Program Logic Models;
2. Evaluation Stakeholders;
3. Evaluation Key Questions;
4. "Best Fit" Evaluation Approach or Model;
5. Timeline and Other Project Management Plans.

It is defined as "the systematic collection of information about the activities, characteristics, and outcomes of programs to make judgments about the program, improve program effectiveness, and/or inform decisions about future programming" (Preskill, and Catsambas, 2006, p. 37). In brief, this is both a critical and essentially vital process which ultimately results in the collection, hence gathering of vital information otherwise necessary for gaining a broader plus more in-depth understanding. This understanding in fact concerns the direct connection or correlation between facilitated actions and the all-encompassing culture.

Program Logic Model (PLM)

The PLM; it "displays what an existing idea, new program, or focused change effort might contain from start to finish" (Knowlton, and Phillips, 2007, p. 36). In other words, the information included within the model's context, in the end, ultimately results in the effectiveness. It also includes the comprehensive design, development, planning, management, and the thorough evaluation of organizational components, information, and fundamentally vital resources thereof. In brief, the PLM, moreover, is comprised of the following core elements or components: 1. Resources; 2. Activities; 3. Outputs; 4. Outcomes; 5. Impact.

The first element—**PLM Resources**; it is considered as the most basic and fundamental components of the overall model. It is considered "essential for activities to occur" (Knowlton, and Phillips, 2007, p. 37). The second element—**PLM Activities**, is the corresponding activities, procedures, or processes which occurs. In brief, it is considered by Knowlton and Phillips (2007) as the "specific actions that make up the program" (p. 37). The third element—**PLM Outputs**, is in fact the end results of activities being actively engaged and performed. In brief, it is considered as the specific offspring from which activities direct results; they are "often quantified and qualified in some way" (Knowlton, and Phillips, 2007, p. 37). The fourth element—**PLM Outcomes**; it is characterized as the resulting change, development, or growth which ultimately results at the latter end of the mode-continuum or pendulum, more like it. It fundamentally involves maturation in "program participants or organizations" (Knowlton, and Phillips, 2007, p. 37). The final element—**PLM Impact**; it is best described as the direct impact which effectuates in the corresponding individual or organizational sphere of influence—locally, regionally, or global context. In brief, it is nothing less than the ongoing and long-lasting change—constructive and destructive, which ultimately results in the end, at the checkered flag, if you prefer.

Evaluation Stakeholders

The stakeholders comprise financial backers, personal, as well as private investors. The specific list includes: 1. Executive Administration; 2. Faculty; 3. Support; 4. Curriculum Designers; 5. Theorists; 6. Staff; 7. Students; 8. Diverse other prospects. As a side bar; evaluation stakeholders are defined by The Joint Committee on Standards for Educational Evaluation (2006) as "those who should be involved in or perhaps even directly affected by the results, one way or the other. In brief, the classification of stake or shareholders is clearly identified, as follows:

- ⅄ Tier one—**primary stakeholders**, which includes students and diverse clients impacted directly by the facilitation of activity;
- ⅄ Tier two—**secondary stakeholder**; includes corporate financial backers, personal and private investors;
- ⅄ Tier three—**tertiary stakeholders**; includes senior-level Executive-level administration, faculty, support staff, curriculum designers, and academic theorists.

QUADRANT III

FIELD OF THE INVENTION

The present invention relates generally to a method, apparatus and system. More specifically, the present invention is a new method and system for higher education.

CONTINUATION—GENESIS OF THE |QUẢNTUM| ACAD(YNA^{E3})MICS$^{SM®}$ Strategic Acadio-sphere

<<Informed Consent Form>>

INTRODUCTION:

The |Quẩntum| Acad(yna^{E3})mics$^{SM®}$ Strategic System. It diligently strives and endeavors to achieve a mission which places *first priority* upon designing and facilitating an academic learning-environment that develops, hence advanced critical thinkers. These students are not only effective, but most importantly balanced between cutting-edge innovation, and pragmatic relevance within the context of a world greatly inundated by a perpetual quandary of crises—challenges, issues, and dilemmas.

It fundamentally encompasses a most comprehensive set of goals, objectives, and core values, all of which places great emphasis upon:

1. **Goals**—develops a system that affords the resources and tools needed for a maximized learning experience;

2. **Values**—students are considered the overarching and underlying reason for engaging in the facilitation of learning, first and foremost.

Effectiveness and quality is valued above speed or expediency of learning facilitation and reception. Instructors are willing, above and beyond, to accommodate students in such a way that it does not compromise the overall integrity of the system itself.

Also, every effort is endeavored to ensure that maximized harmony plus synergy is a reality between all corresponding participants; this includes administration, faculty, staff, and student learners. Thus, it is a diligent effort to continue providing high quality resources to the body of students.

Next, an organized tutoring program is developed; this ensures that those students whom are experiencing difficulties will be afforded the necessary critical assistance.

Anyhow, the following information is provided to you—prospect student and participant, in an effort to decide whether you wish to actively participate in this overall study. The administration, faculty, and staff of TQASS strongly support and adhere to the protection of human subjects participating in this research experience.

You may, in fact, refuse to sign this consent form, and opt not to participate therein. There are no existing penalties, or negative affects in your relationship with TQASS. In brief, if you agree to participate in this research program, know that you are free to withdraw at any time whatsoever.

PURPOSE OF THE STUDY:

The overarching purpose of this study is to evaluate the effectiveness of the comprehensive virtual learning program, and its full utilization of innovative study modalities, strategies, and techniques.

PROCEDURES:

You may be asked to participate in a focus group or complete a survey, of perhaps even both. Focus groups may last from 1-10 hours, on approximately. The focus group sessions will be audio recorded and transcribed. The questionnaire will take fifteen minutes, approximately.

All tapes, surveys, and transcriptions will be stored in a locked cabinet in the research office of TQASS, with exclusive access afforded only to applicable researchers and staff.

Findings of the interviews and surveys will generate a final report to be shared with all corresponding-levels of TQASS.

RISKS:

"As with any innovative system which fundamentally proposes increased efficacy and quality germane to success for averting otherwise unforeseen crises. As with any next-generation system, there exist "moderate risks". However, if integrated skillfully and systematically as the author postulates and thus instructs, the volume of crises will be significantly reduced if not totally averted!" In brief, there is no guarantee that All crises will be fully avoided. This is our guarantee. The amount of crises will be greatly reduced and its overall negative consequences.

BENEFITS:

TQASS will be able to validate the need and effectiveness of comprehensive learning plus tutoring program. Both students and TQASS will see increased success pertinent to those whom the complete breadth and length of this comprehensive academic-learning program.

PAYMENT TO PARTICIPANTS:

The total payment for active participation within the context of this research is $35 hourly, for each participant respectively.

PARTICIPANT CONFIDENTIALITY:

Your name will not be associated in any way with the information collected or in the research findings. A numbered coding system will replace your name to eliminate any risk of confidentiality compromise. The researchers will not share any information about you, of course only if required by law or with written permission.

Permission granted on this date to use and disclose your information remains in effect indefinitely. In signing this form, rest assured, you are giving permission for use and disclosure of your information for the purpose of this study.

QUESTIONS REGARDING PARTICIPATION:

Questions about procedures or participation can be directed to the researcher listed at the end of this consent form.

PARTICIPANT CERTIFICATION:

I have read this Consent and Authorization Form. Opportunity as been given to me to ask questions, and I have adequately received answers to any questions I have regarding this study. I understand that if I have any additional questions about my rights as a research participant, or my change in participation, I can call (469) 226-3103—official number to be determined, or write to the recognized auditing staff of TQASS @ _____ (Official physical location and address, yet to be determined), or email at claude.e.bonet2020@gmail.com; note, this is indeed subject to change.

In closing, I agree to actively participate in this research study. By my signature, I am verifying that I am at least 18 years of age.

I also acknowledge that I have received a copy of this Consent and Authorization Form.

Intuitively Yours,

XXXXX

_____

Print Participant's Name Date

_____

Participant's Signature

Section Four: Interview Survey Section (ISS)

The ISS is the aspect or component which concentrates primarily upon both the presentation of the hypothetical cover letter, and the physical submission of the actual survey questionnaire. The fundamental purpose for the *cover letter component* is to provide an introductory-based correspondence which essentially affords the recipient a succinct, yet somewhat comprehensive listing of all the relevant intricacies and particulars involved in the overall survey. It not only lists all that entails the survey, but also highlights the underlying significance for engaging therein the process, from the outset.

Next, pertinent to the fundamental purpose of the survey questionnaire, it essentially lists the diverse questions considered as most vital and relevant towards the context of the overall study.

In brief, it affords a series of questions which attempts to measure not only the current status of the overall organizational system, rather most importantly the actual nuts and bolts required for improving the overall systemic quality.

Example Cover Letter (hypothetical):

The |Quåntum| Acad(yna^{E3})mics$^{SM®}$ Strategic System
(Physical Address and Location; yet to be Determined)
Cedar Hill, TX 75104-5115

June 2013
Mr. Optimistic One Prospect
John Doe, Jr.
1234 Inquisitive Minded Blvd.
Perception, TX 75104-0000

Ms. Prospect:

Welcome to this wondrous opportunity for constructively impacting the overall quality of learning which is afforded to all of the students of The |Quåntum| Acad(ynaE3)mics Strategic System—past, present, and future context. In our opinion, you have indeed made the right decision in becoming an active participant in the development and facilitation of academics, all of which originates at this cutting-edge institute for higher learning.

Anyhow, we—the executive staff and administration team of The |Quåntum| Acad(yna^{E3}) mics$^{SM®}$ Strategic System want to take this moment and extend our hands of appreciation for your willingness to participate in this most important matter. We understand how challenging and difficult it might be to set aside and this sacrifice valuable time away from your usual schedule.

In brief, we believe and are most confident that this experience will be, if nothing else, a most richly rewarding learning opportunity; an experience that will greatly benefit many vast parties. In addition, it must be stated that every opportunity has been invested in ensuring that this overall experience sets the stage for addressing and thus acquiring as much relevant plus vital information which only contributes towards the quality of learning which is afforded to each and every student which applies, registers for, and thus enrolls in pursuit of their higher academic matriculation, here at the academy.

Rest assured each and every piece of information that has been afforded and rightly responded to will be given much attention. It will also be afforded in-depth comprehensive dialogue, expression, and insightful plus intuitive reflection. Once this stage has been officially completed, the necessary subsequent steps will be employed in ensuring that the future facilitation of learning will be acutely reflective thereof.

In closing, the attached survey form outlines the details of what we'll do and how successful we have been at doing this activity for other diverse clients. In the end, you can be fully ensured n knowing that all of your feedback and candid insights plus opinions, is literally serving to improve the overall academic-quality of life, which has yet to be experienced by a generation of leaders, thinkers, and scholars whom have yet to be fully conceived or even realized thereof.

Thanks in advance, for your time and unwavering consideration!

If there are any questions; please do not hesitate, we can be reached directly at:

1. (469) 226-3103—official too-free number, yet to be determined;
2. Write to the recognized auditing staff of TQASS @ _____ (Official physical location and address, yet to be determined);
3. Email at claude.e.bonet2020@gmail.com. Notice, it is subject to change, TBD!

Cordially, Yours,
Prof Claude E. Bonet
469/226-3103 direct
claude.e.bonet2020@gmail.com email

President/ Founder/ CIO

Enclosure: 1 Cover Letter &

Survey Questionnaire:

Survey Questionnaire	Strongly Agree = '1'	Agree = '2'	Neutral = '3'	Disagree = '4'	Strongly Agree = '5'	N/A/ = '6'

[Questions]

I am familiar with the overall mission of TQASS.

The participant is an alumnus of TQASS.

A few weaknesses or deficiencies have been identified.

A few strengths or assets have been identified.

I agree with the current strategies facilitated by TQASS.

I will invest monies and resources in full support of the Vision of TQASS.

The overall experience has greatly benefited the participant's life and career.

Regarding future training, in pursuit of higher-level credentials, TQASS is at the top of the list.

Essential information, resources, and tools have been increasingly afforded since the first and initial encounter.

The overall quality of TQASS is such that it prepares its students to be not only effective, but also wholly plus soundly balanced professional.